Parenting an Adult
with Disabilities
or Special Needs

Parenting an Adult with Disabilities or Special Needs

Everything You Need to Know to Plan for and Protect Your Child's Future

Peggy Lou Morgan

New York ▪ Atlanta ▪ Brussels ▪ Chicago ▪ Mexico City
San Francisco ▪ Shanghai ▪ Tokyo ▪ Toronto ▪ Washington, D.C.

Special discounts on bulk quantities of AMACOM books are available to corporations, professional associations, and other organizations. For details, contact Special Sales Department, AMACOM, a division of American Management Association, 1601 Broadway, New York, NY 10019.
Tel: 212-903-8316. Fax: 212-903-8083.
E-mail: specialsls@amanet.org
Website: www.amacombooks.org/go/specialsales
To view all AMACOM titles go to: www.amacombooks.org

This publication is designed to provide accurate and authoritative information in regard to the subject matter covered. It is sold with the understanding that the publisher is not engaged in rendering legal, accounting, or other professional service. If legal advice or other expert assistance is required, the services of a competent professional person should be sought.

Library of Congress Cataloging-in-Publication Data

Morgan, Peggy Lou, 1950-
    Parenting an adult with disabilities or special needs : everything you need to know to plan for and protect your child's future / Peggy Lou Morgan.
        p. cm.
    Includes bibliographical references and index.
    ISBN-13: 978-0-8144-0991-6 (pbk.)
    ISBN-10: 0-8144-0991-1 (pbk.)
    1. Parents of children with disabilities.   2. People with disabilities—Services for.   3. Parent and adult child.   4. Parenting. I. Title.

    HQ759.913.M68 2009
    649'.151—dc22

                                            2008033521

Printing number
10 9 8 7 6 5 4 3 2 1

For

Raymond A. Jones, Jr., our pastor, friend, and encourager
during some of the most difficult times Billy Ray
and I have experienced;

William E. Brown, my agent who taught me how to put
my thoughts in marketable form and use the Internet
to help get my message out, and who found me
such a wonderful publisher;

Ellen Kadin, at AMACOM Books, my wonderful editor
and very special friend, who has taught
this inexperienced author so much
about publishing and how to get the message
of encouragement out to parents;

Bud Pugh, my teacher, spiritual advisor, friend, and encourager,
who taught me so much about public speaking; and

Richard Lighthill, our pastor and friend, who is always
there for Billy Ray and me.

CONTENTS

CHAPTER 4

CHAPTER 5

CHAPTER 6

CHAPTER 7

FOREWORD

Peggy Morgan and I have been sharing our ideas and reflections as well as the daily grind of our lives over the past several years. We are like bookends holding the experience of families living with disability throughout America. Peggy lives in Oregon and corresponds through her website with families throughout the United States and the world, while I live in New York City and support diverse people with disabilities and their families to reach for the best possible lives they can create for themselves. I have worked for 35 years as a professional in the field of disabilities, promoting the values and possibilities related to person-centered work, and I'm also the sister of a brother with complex medical and support needs. Peggy is mother to Billy Ray, a thinker and writer about parenting children with special needs, and a former professional fiduciary. While far apart in circumstance, we see possibilities for people with disabilities through the same lens, and these shared views are the focus of this book.

I love *Parenting an Adult with Disabilities or Special Needs: Everything You Need to Know to Plan for and Protect Your Child's Future*, because Peggy gets to the heart of the complexity of the task of planning for the future with compassion, common sense, attention to detail, and deep wisdom. As a parent, you will journey with Peggy through your deepest fears related to "what will happen when I'm gone," to practical advice about day-to-day implementation of both immediate and long-range plans that create the best life possible for your child and yourself, even in the face of the overwhelming demands and relentless challenges of daily life. Peggy does not offer a quick fix or easy answers; instead, she shares the difficult chapters, hard-earned triumphs, and lessons learned from her own life, and her experience with families and professionals throughout the world.

In some ways, 2008 is the best of times for people with disabilities and their families. More than ever in history, people with even the most severe disabilities are working in and contributing to community life; they are serving in leadership roles in both civic life and self-advocacy associations. Some people are becoming well-known as artists, musicians, poets, and in other fields of creative arts; people are involved in and inspiring spiritual communities; they are getting married, living in and/or owning their own homes; and many people are self-directing their supports by charting their own futures: hiring the people who support them, and managing their own budgets and affairs. Many families have more support than ever: in home, after school, and weekend support, respite care, year-round school options, and membership opportunities in parent support and advocacy groups.

Consequently, it is a brave new world for people with disabilities, made so by their courage and the activism of families who have led the way to social change and new opportunities. In these best-case scenarios, people with disabilities, their families, community members, and professionals are creating these new worlds of possibility together, regardless of the level of disability and supports needed.

On the other hand, for others, now is the worst of times. Many people with disabilities are segregated and congregated in service environments that restrict and limit their potential. They and their families depend on government service dollars that can be overwhelmingly complicated, restrictive, and/or increasingly difficult to obtain. Many states have incredibly long waiting lists for essential supports, which leave people isolated at home and their families in despair. Many, many students who are entitled to an inclusive educational experience and a transition to a productive adult life graduate at age 21 without community experience, job skills and opportunities, and other essential supports.

Civil rights laws exist to create opportunities, but without the vigilant activism of parents, injustice goes unexamined and unchallenged. This book reminds family members that they must be the champions for change for their loved ones. In the face of daily hardship, family members are still the most likely force for positive change for their own children and for the collective status of all people with disabilities.

PARENTS WILL ALWAYS BE THE STRONGEST ANCHORS, ALLIES, TEACHERS, AND LEADERS

Peggy Morgan challenges families to see the highest future possibility for their loved ones and to find allies who will hold onto these hopes. Marginalized people, particularly people with disabilities, are habitually not recognized and not referred to in terms of their capacities and future potential.

This book addresses the critical role families can serve in seeing family members in light of their capacities, holding onto their dreams for a good life, and putting ideals into action while they are still able to do so. Strategies are provided—such as writing your child's story from a capacity view, looking for the hidden dream, supporting siblings to be champions, and creating and implementing powerful transitional plans.

A focus on job development and employment is a critical aspect of creating the dream. I agree with Peggy that parents can be catalysts for effective job development and support. Washington State provides us with an illuminating model of the impact of believing that all people with disabilities can work. Washington has demonstrated the power of aligning policies to support work experience during high school, to provide customized adult supports that continue the dream, and to address the disincentives to work described in this book. Washington State has achieved astonishing levels of employment for all people with disabilities, regardless of challenge. Employment is one of the highest future possibilities for people with disabilities, and families can begin facilitating this vision when a child is just 12 to 14 years old.

However, the dreams that parents hold for their children are far more complex than just employment; Peggy addresses the core issue of safeguarding quality of life by discussing the very messy business of relationship building. We know from experience that *who* is in the life of our loved ones matters more that *what* is on paper, and so a vibrant transition plan is a life-long creative process of building and strengthening relationships with others who will be there, to hold and to carry the dreams, hardships, and vulnerabilities that people bring.

Of course, effective parenting and long-term planning includes wills, trusts, representatives, guardians, and attorneys, and Peggy outlines concise and helpful roadmaps from the perspective of a parent who has worked as a fiduciary. I greatly appreciate the constant theme and continued encouragement to families to "build a circle" of all kinds of people in all kinds of roles who will act individually and collectively to protect, nurture, and watch over the quality of life created while parents are able to do so, so that quality is sustained beyond the parent's ability to be the champion. This is the ultimate gift a parent can give to a vulnerable child, and this book describes the essence and nature of that gift.

In summary, I know that Peggy and I both wish we could say to parents that services and systems will provide for your child; if only we all had enough services, then everything would be fine. Certainly, good supports can help, and they can make a huge difference in the quality of life for your child and your family. But ultimately, the qualities that people bring to people with disabilities and that people with disabilities bring into the world can never be mandated, regulated, or required by systems. These qualities—passion, hope, concern, commitment, devotion, responsiveness, inspiration, loyalty, integrity—must be recognized, encouraged, and strengthened. This book calls out the best in us as fellow humans—family members, community members, and committed workers—to work together to build a better world for people with disabilities, and in doing so we build a better world for us all.

Beth Mount, PhD
October 2008

ACKNOWLEDGMENTS

It would be impossible to name everyone who has made a difference in getting this book out. There are so many.

I dedicated my first book to Billy Ray, so it seemed inappropriate to do that again; however, I must say that without my son there would be nothing to share. He continues to be the best teacher I could have. My husband, Larry, and our large extended families have been a major help. Thank you to my own parents, Ron and Daisy Waterhouse, and to the best mother-in-law you could have for their encouragement.

Many people at AMACOM Books have become like family. There is a sense that we have done something special together every time I get an email from a parent who has been helped by my writing. Included in this AMACOM family is Matt Hickey, who left AMACOM Books to return to school but had such a major part in teaching me promotions and still checks in with much encouragement from time to time.

I would be remiss not to mention our special friends, Donna and Max Hoffman. Whether it is inquiring about how many pages I have written that day or making high-fiber cookies for Billy Ray, they are always there for us. Your love for us is amazing. Also Pastor Lighthill and the congregation of our little Grace Fellowship Church of the Nazarene have been supportive and encouraging at every step. Just to describe the love and support would fill many pages.

Big thanks to Beth Mount, PhD, for allowing me to use her term Loneliness Is the Only Real Disability and for her encouragement, as well as for writing the foreword.

Parenting an Adult with Disabilities or Special Needs

INTRODUCTION

In the preface for my first book, *Parenting Your Complex Child*,[1] I compared life with a special needs child to a war with many battlefields. You may think that transitioning into adulthood for your child will be less of a combat zone. Sorry to burst your balloon. It can be the same war with more battlefields because more governmental agencies are involved in providing services and support to adults with disabilities than to children.

In 1994 Joseph Shapiro wrote *No Pity: People with Disabilities Forging a New Civil Rights Movement*,[2] which shared the stories of people who had struggled for their rights despite disabilities. In 1990 the Americans with Disabilities Act (ADA) was enacted. Yet, in 2006, I wrote:

> Disabled persons have equal access to all public places [that] is guaranteed under the Americans with Disabilities Act. We aren't locking all disabled persons away anymore. Yet when I take my son out in public and everyone stares, I find myself looking around and wondering, "Where are his peers?" He is often the only developmentally disabled person we see in restaurants, various types of stores, and even our church.
>
> Taking our complex children out in the community can be hard work. Just getting out the door can be exhausting. If your child is loud

or disruptive, the public can be vicious. The question of whether it is worth the bother is always in the forefront.[3]

Public transportation and sidewalks are more wheelchair-accessible in some areas. Other areas, such as New York City and Bend, Oregon, are still very much in need of accessibility. And the public itself is not necessarily more accepting. I see fewer people with disabilities working in offices, grocery stores, or restaurants, even though they may enjoy the work more than other employees. Recently I overheard a bank manager and a local business owner discussing how difficult it was to keep good employees. In our area, which is big on skiing and other tourist attractions, surely people with disabilities could be recruited for many jobs. As we will see, it might be more than lack of recruitment on the part of employers.

Eighteen years after the enactment of the ADA, you would expect to see more and more people with disabilities in the community, not fewer and fewer.

In a recent conversation with Andrew Houtenville, of Cornell University's Rehabilitation Research and Training Center on Demographics and Statistics, he described SSI (Supplemental Security Income) and SSDI (Social Security Disability Income) as being "institutionalism in the home." In other words, many things such as medical care, housing, food stamps, and other services for disabled persons are tied to one's eligibility for SSI. If one risks losing his SSI by earning enough money to be disqualified from the benefit, he also risks losing other life-sustaining services such as medication, healthcare, and in-home assistance. Incentives to try to create a fulfilling life are hampered greatly by such policies.

I wrote a second book because my son, Billy Ray, now 26 years old, is at this transition stage in his life. I wanted to share the complexities that he and others who experience disabilities will go through. Hopefully, this new book will help other parents prepare for the family transition process.

I laughed to my wonderful editor, Ellen Kadin at AMACOM Books, that maybe I shouldn't write any more books. After the first book had gone to the publisher, Billy Ray experienced a health crisis. My editor encouraged me to add information about that crisis to the first book. I experienced a crisis near the end of writing this book. On New Year's Eve 2007, I experienced breathing problems and was rushed to the hospital. During the ambulance ride, the EMT told me that if I didn't slow down my breathing, I might not make it to the hospital. All I could think about was my son Billy

Ray's transition to adulthood—and everything about it that had yet to be done. Again, I dealt with that nagging question: What will happen to Billy Ray when I die? Again, it gave me something to add to what I had written.

Maybe like me you think that you have made all the arrangements to protect your adult child. Periodic review of the options may show more that you can do to protect him or find more opportunities for him.

It may seem easiest just to keep your adult child at home with you, where he is safe and happy. The difficult transition may not seem worth it. But it shouldn't take a wakeup call like mine to realize that he will likely survive you. Unless you do something about it, he will be unprepared to leave the nest you have created for him. Plus, he has a right to as fulfilling a life as possible. So the most loving thing you can do for him is to prepare him to fly from the nest. That does not mean that you will dump him out of the nest before he is ready or you have found (or created) an appropriate adult situation. It means that you will do all that you can to prepare for that event even if you are not available to participate in his transition.

Sometimes the struggle seems overwhelming. But the alternative is not desirable: You could keep your adult child at home until you can no longer assist him. If no transition planning is done, the chances are your county or state agency will place him wherever they have a slot available. It will not necessarily be the ideal for him as an individual, which may add frustration to his loneliness over not being with you.

It has probably taken you years to become the expert on your child. You know what his behaviors mean, and you automatically respond in the appropriate way. You know how to maintain his environment and routine in order to avoid confusion, which has an impact on his ability to go with the flow rather than have a meltdown out of confusion. You'll need to preserve this expertise for the transition process.

There is a tendency for others who don't know your child as well as you to deal with withdrawal or behavior problems with medication to make someone with disabilities more "manageable." I believe that a lot of behavior issues are caused by what I call "communication by behavior." (In his writing and presentations, "difficult behavior" expert Dr. David Pitonyak refers to it as "messages," but the principle is the same). The behavior is a communication that something isn't working for the person. It could be an environmental issue, a physical problem, or an inability to communicate something that is bothering him. It may have taken you much of his life to figure out what works best. If he were placed in a facility or group home where staff didn't have the benefit of your knowledge, the chance is high that his behavior will be seen as just undesirable behavior, not as communication. And, rather than "listening" to what's being communicated by behavior and maybe finding a solution to a problem, medication to control the behavior may be prescribed.

I am not anti-medication, but finding solutions first is always desirable, if possible. My advice is to document the "communication by behavior" you have discovered over the years and solutions you have created for dealing with the issues. Then train assistants, job coaches, and others how to respond to specific behaviors.

Like anyone else, regardless of disability, your adult child will undoubtedly experience disappointments in life. On the other hand, by taking a proactive stance in transition planning, things will be much better than if no steps are taken. The panic surrounding that nagging question will be substantially reduced.

Several years ago, I was privileged to hear Dr. David Pitonyak at a conference where we were both speaking. He gave a handout entitled "Loneliness Is the Only Real Disability." That phrase has haunted me ever since, because I have seen the loneliness of many people who experience disabilities.

There are many things that we as parents can do to make a difference in our children's transition to adulthood. However, even if we can do nothing else but plan to avoid the loneliness, we will have accomplished much. Perhaps having long-term nurturing and healing relationships may be even more important than finding the most ideal work or residential experience.

Thus, instead of getting stuck on what we can't do because of red tape or lack of resources, we can move forward and accomplish things together with our adult children. We can find the peace that comes from dealing with the nagging question of what happens to him when we are gone because we have been proactive in creating safeguards and protections for him.

Some adult children may continue on to college or vocational training. Others may try to merge into the community through meaningful employment. Compared to school settings, each of these options brings significantly increased challenges and perhaps even more prejudice and lack of acceptance.

When your child was in school, you probably had IEP (Individual Education Plan) team meetings. These may have been filled with conflict regarding the appropriate education for your child. In most areas, the same team concept applies to services for adults. The team may be smaller than the IEP team. Like the IEP team, its purpose is to create a plan and goals for care and service, this time for an *adult* with disabilities. This is often referred to as an "Individual Service Plan" or ISP. Other agencies such as Social Security, the Housing Authority, and Vocational Rehabilitation may not get directly involved with the ISP team, but you still may need to interact with them because they provide services to your adult child.

There is another significant battlefield in planning for adults with disabilities: legislation intended to help people who experience disabilities with support and medical care, etc. Instead what they have created is a "poverty track," according to David C. Stapleton, Center for Studying Disability Policy, Mathemetica Policy Research.[4]

Because of the lack of opportunities for adults with disabilities, it is not unusual for an adult child to still be at home with his parents when they are elderly. Transition will be smoother and more successful for an adult with disabilities when it occurs during his parents' lifetime—and when the parent are still able to participate in it.

What is a parent to do? Actually, there are numerous things that will make a real difference in your adult child's transition to adulthood. It may feel hopeless, but you need not accept defeat and give up. You can be proactive. It doesn't require a PhD (although you will learn a lot) and it's not combat duty (although you'll face battles of a different sort).

Team-building advocacy for your adult child is just as important, if not more so, than when he was a child in school. You can make it a war, or you can work to build a team that will accomplish things for your adult child.

Appendix C contains an article entitled "Team-Building Advocacy" from my website, www.parentingyourcomplexchild.com. It addresses children, not adults, but the principles of team building are applicable and you may find it helpful.

Red tape and policies are confusing to begin with. Disability laws can be even more so, because they differ from state to state. The Social Security Act provides that monies will be disbursed to states according to state-created plans with SSA approval. However, to receive services, federal regulations must also be met.

Buried in the regulations are conditions and loopholes that may actually enable opportunities, but they can be hard to find. A case manager in another area recently told me that she occasionally finds loopholes by accident—and that they make a difference for her client. Other times, she said, parents find programs and loopholes that will work for their children. In other words, working together as a team for the greatest benefit of your adult child can make a genuine difference in his success.

When your child was in school, you needed to know about education laws. Now you'll need to know about laws regarding government benefits, equal access, employment opportunities, and more. And in addition to understanding individual areas of law, you'll need to know about how some services can offset other services—and how that could disqualify your adult child from receiving important benefits.

When I wrote the proposal for my first book, there weren't nearly as many books by parents about parenting a child with special needs. Now there are many such books. It is interesting how many of us have very different experiences and insights. That is likely because we are different people and our children are individuals. As much as some would like to believe, there is no such thing as a typical person with special needs.

There are varying messages on parenting a child or adult who experiences some type of disability. I come not to criticize other messages. Instead, I want to share my thoughts regarding:

- People who experience disabilities have just as much right to "life, liberty, and the pursuit of happiness" as any other person.
- The joy that comes from knowing you helped your child achieve goals that had been considered unachievable because of society's low expectations for people with disabilities.
- The peace that comes from feeling you have put protections in place so that one day your adult child will be understood and cared for as close as possible to how you cared for him during your lifetime.

Society doesn't see your child the way you do. Too often others see only the disability, not the abilities and not the personality. What your child can achieve with a few adaptations, some of them very minor, is hidden to most people. This is worsened by well-meaning persons and organizations attempting to raise funds for research or other causes who actually paint a child or adult with disabilities in the worst light. Disabilities are exaggerated and abilities are ignored.

I believe an important part of our role as parents is to try to present our children as the people they truly are. Until society has a genuine awareness of the value of each and every person with disabilities, a movement for change will never take place. When it comes, the change will not come out of pity, but understanding and acceptance.

When nothing was working for Billy Ray, I devoured every book I could get my hands on, and everything on the Internet that I could find. Nothing fit exactly, but I gleaned things from many authors and adapted them to come up with what worked best for Billy Ray. The various points of view and suggestions, combined with what I already knew worked for Billy Ray, jump-started my creativity to design systems for him. As I read, I gained greater understanding for Billy Ray. Sometimes it was like a light bulb going off: I would say, "Ah-ha! That's why he behaves that way!" But that didn't necessarily mean that the methods suggested in those articles or books worked for Billy Ray. I would have to take whatever insights I gleaned and adapt solutions to what would work for him.

My son is not exactly like your child or adult child. What works for him may not work for everyone. It is my hope that you will find something in this book that will be helpful to you in adapting what will work for your child or adult child's transition planning. I hope that it will jump-start your creativity as others' works have done for me over the years.

HOW CAN THIS BOOK HELP?

All parents deal with the sometimes-paralyzing question of what happens to adult children when we can no longer be there for them. While legal documents are very important, they may not prepare caregivers, nominated representatives, or others to understand someone who may not be able to communicate his needs directly. We will deal with that in Chapter 2, "That Nagging Question."

There is much that we can do to assure the continuing support and care for adult children. It takes planning and work but brings a reassuring peace that we have provided everything we could for the time. It provides a protection long after we are unable to provide it in person.

In Chapter 3, "Loneliness Is the Only Real Disability," we will talk about building relationships that will endure beyond your ability to be as involved. We will also talk about the importance of maintaining your child's story. This can make a major difference. Yet, it may not be something parents think about.

In Chapter 4, "Your Child's Pursuit of Happiness," we talk about your child's rights to pursue what will make him happy. Then in Chapter 5, "Discovering Your Child's Dream," we will work through his dreams and identify his natural skills. Also, we'll create a transition planning file.

Transitional programs in school or vocational agencies may not be available until your child is 16 years of age—or even older. By doing some exploring, parents can gain valuable time to help a child determine what kind of life he wants as an adult. If certain skills are needed, they may be learned at home or added to the school IEP if they're thought of early enough.

When Billy Ray was little, I noticed that "sorting skills" were constantly added to his IEP. When I questioned that, I was told it was because his most likely employment as an adult would be in a sheltered workshop, and sorting was an important skill. When it remained for several years after I felt he had mastered it, I was basically given the same explanation. His future seemed preplanned before he had a chance to show us what he would like to do with his life. Looking at it in these two chapters may help avoid having him stuck in the "most likely employment" trap—and allow time to work toward his dream.

Certainly, some things he might like to do will be be unrealistic. However, many things can be accomplished with planning and exploration of programs and services that might relate to his dream. We will talk about that in Chapter 6, "Researching the Options."

In my first book, I discussed creating a transition plan. We will look at that in more detail in Chapter 7, "Drafting a Transitional Plan."

The transitional plan we create in Chapter 7 involves long-term goals that require short-term steps. In Chapter 8, "Setting Goals to Accomplish the Transitional Plan," we will work through creating short-term goals.

In Chapter 9, "Estate Planning," we discuss the various roles of representatives for your adult child. This will help prepare you for planning with your attorney. Additionally, we discuss supplemental information that needs to be available in an estate-planning file in addition to the estate planning documents prepared by your attorney. We will talk about how to glean records and use tools to make information on your adult child's present care and medical history accessible in case you are unavailable when it is needed.

In Chapter 10, "Working with Your Attorney," we talk about establishing a relationship with your attorney and gathering information your attorney will need.

In Chapter 11, "Implementing the Plan a Step at a Time," we talk about getting started in guiding your child through this transition. We also talk about the difficulty this might bring for us as parents. We have cared for our son or daughter, and it is difficult sometimes to step back and teach independence, even if it is a realistic plan.

Transition can be bumpy. You will likely need to be involved as much as possible even after the plan is actually in place. We will discuss your followup in Chapter 12, "The Nest May Seem Empty but You Aren't Done Yet."

In Chapter 13, "Continuing the Civil Rights Movement for Disability Rights," we will discuss ways to bring awareness and advocate for appropriate rights for people who experience special needs.

If you'd like to follow our progress, please check www.peggyloumorgan.com for a list of my websites and blogs. There will be articles on the websites and general venting on my blogs. I would like to say that I will answer all your emails. I really do try! But sometimes I will answer frequently asked questions in a blog post rather than in individual emails. However, I want you to feel free to write me. I may not have the answers, but I can share your frustrations.

Peggy Lou Morgan
www.peggyloumorgan.com
complexmom@gmail.com
LaPine, Oregon

CHAPTER

1

THE NEST IS NEVER EMPTY

AN EMPTY BEDROOM DOES NOT CLEAR THE NEST IN YOUR HEART

From the time you first brought your child home, either as a warm bundle of joy or an older child you adopted, you have worked to make things just right for her. If she experiences special needs, the journey may have had lots of frustrations as well as the joy of discovering things that work for her.

Along the way, you have discovered things that can affect her ability to function during her day. Confusion over what to expect in her schedule may send her into a meltdown. So to avoid her flopping on the floor and refusing to get onto the school bus or into the car, you have learned to help her maintain a planner or picture schedule that works just right for her. Maybe she can't tolerate certain foods or detergents or the irritation from tags in her clothing; or clutter lying around; or the house too hot or too cold, too noisy or too quiet. You recognize that certain changes in her behavior mean she is experiencing a headache or about to start her menstrual cycle. It is probably second nature to you by now but may not be obvious to others she will come into contact with in her adult life.

As parents, we hope to teach our children to take care of themselves. We dream of our children flying from the nest fully prepared for a whole new life on their own. We want them to be able to stand independently after they leave. When they are able to take care of themselves, you will have more time for yourself. You can take some classes or learn to golf. Maybe your child's old bedroom will become the craft room you've always wanted.

As parents of a child with special needs, we too may gain that extra bedroom one day, but the nest may never be empty. Considering our extraordinary caregiving and responsibility, we live with the question of what happens to our children when we are no longer here to make sure they are taken care of. We think we have everything worked out, but then a skills trainer or support staff quits, a program ends, etc., etc. And once again we face the added responsibility.

Transition to adult life is complicated whether your nearly adult child is higher functioning or lower functioning. Things may seem to be working well in her home, but havoc may be lurking just below the surface. Suddenly a crisis can develop in her adult home—seemingly without warning.

If your child is ready for transition to adult living, the chances are you have spent the past nearly two decades figuring out how to adapt to what works for her as an individual. This is probably true regardless of whether she experiences disabilities. She is a unique person who can function best if things are done a certain way for her. Much of it may be second nature to both of you because it is how you have done things for a long time. That's why your input is vital to her successful transition to adulthood.

Adults may be perfectly capable of becoming self-advocates. At the same time, there is a lot to learn about policies and regulations for the various programs that are available. She will need support in learning how to research programs and advocate for herself without becoming so frustrated she gives up. The amount of support you need to provide will probably decrease eventually, but it may be necessary for long periods of time.

In reality, many adults who experience disabilities may never be totally independent. If your adult child is high functioning and transitioning into an independent living situation, there can still be a multitude of issues she will need support with. This is a big step for her. Maybe she can cook for herself but not handle finances. Or maybe she can write her own checks to pay bills and buy her own groceries, but must learn to live within her budget. Others may need a part-time or full-time assistant in their own home. Still others require more structured residential and vocational program as adults.

Jokes about the grown child (usually without disabilities) who never leaves the nest abound. For an adult child with disabilities this may be reality. There are multiple complications in trying to ensure that your child will have a safe and happy adult life when you are no longer able to care for her. Vocational, residential, and other services to adults are not necessarily immediately available upon graduation from high school. On average, an adult child with disabilities leaves her family's home much later than an adult child who does not experience disabilities. These adult children also return to live at home more often than adult children without disabilities.

If your adult child has moved into her own home with support staff that is full- or part-time, there may be high turnover. Parents are usually involved in training new staff: You might actually conduct the training, arrange for it, or somehow fund the transition because government funds may not be available.

Unless you are able to have an agency that provides staff, you may spend time with her when her support staff person has an appointment or calls in sick or, worse yet, quits without notice. The nest may not always be in your home, but your involvement in keeping it warm and safe may continue forever.

The media is full of stories we don't want to think about—vulnerable adults being abused or exploited. You wonder how you can protect her from everything, especially when you are not able to be involved in the same way you are now. Helping her build relationships that will continue beyond your ability to stay involved will add protection. We will discuss those protections in Chapter 3, "Loneliness Is the Only Real Disability."

If you visit residential and vocational programs, you will likely see people who don't seem happy in those settings. While person-centered planning is discussed more and more, there are still areas that push clients into existing systems instead of trying to create what works for the individual.

In the not-so-distant past, children and adults with disabilities—especially the more severe diagnoses—were placed in state-run or state-supported institutional settings. Often, they never really nested in the home to begin with. Parents were told to place them in an institution and not get too attached. We have come a long way from those times. Yet, a lingering effect is that the *abilities* of those experiencing disabilities remain somewhat hidden. As a society we may provide better care, but we still don't provide the opportunities for a happy, fulfilling life because we don't see abilities, only *disabilities*.

Those big institutions have been closing and bringing their residents into the community. While it is a wonderful trend, communities and programs are often unequipped to deal with the needs of their new community members. This is complicated by the increased occurrence of conditions such as autism, which is being diagnosed more and more frequently.

Even before the institutions began closing, children and adults who were already in the community often had to fight for services such as residential and/or vocational programs. Now, community resources that are already stretched must cover even more people with disabilities. For many communities, it has been difficult to keep up with services.

Unless your adult child is able to work to support herself financially or adequate private family funding is available, the chances are good she will need some assistance from governmental programs. This can require long waiting lists both for vocational and residential services.

Sometimes these waiting lists are "crisis driven." For example, the waiting list may be twenty to thirty years or even longer. If the parent or caregiver becomes unable to continue caring for an adult child, she will be considered "in crisis." Thus, she will be moved up to the top of the list. Otherwise, she'll maintain her place on the list.

In our own state, Oregon, there was a class action lawsuit in 2000 by Medicaid-eligible adults with special needs who had spent many years on waiting lists for services. The case was settled with what has come be known at the Staley Settlement Agreement. It provides for limited services to eligible persons and increased residential services by 2009. According to the settlement, top priority for services will be given to persons whose primary caregiver is over 75 years of age.

I believe the persons involved in this Settlement Agreement were already in the community and not residents of the institution that—interestingly enough—also closed in 2000. It appears that community services may have been inadequate even before the institution closed. The addition of the residents from the institution exacerbated the shortage of resources considerably.

Unfortunately, due to unavailability of appropriate resources, it is quite common for parents to have their adult children with special needs at home until the parents are elderly. The children remain there until the parents can no longer take care of them because of death, illness, or incapacity. Once it reaches that point, important information about the children's needs and histories may be irretrievable from the parents. For example, if a parent has Alzheimer's, it may be impossible for her to answer important questions that her adult child cannot answer about her care or medical history.

If she remains at home with you until you are no longer able to participate in planning, chances are greater that she will be put in whatever vocational and/or residential program is available rather than one where she'll be happy. That is frightening. You can overcome some of the fear by being proactive in planning. You can even put the long wait for services to good use: For example, use the time to help her learn to become a self-advocate, or you can involve someone you believe will be a powerful advocate when you can no longer do so.

The concept of person-centered planning has been around for many years. Basically, it means allowing the person to be involved in creating a happy life for herself. Many agencies and programs support the concept in word, but not in practice. Unfortunately, it is easier and cheaper to do things the way they've always been done. Also, there is often a lack of true understanding of the capabilities of an individual with disabilities.

In her book *Person-Centered Planning: Finding Directions for Change Using Personal Futures Planning,*[5] Beth Mount compares "system centered" to "person centered." System-centered planning is structured to meet the needs of the system more than the individual. Obviously, it is going to be easier and cheaper for the system to create programs that are larger than several smaller ones that are adapted to individuals.

You are the expert in your child or adult child. You know better than anyone else what she can do. The likelihood of determining what will make her happy is greater if you are involved. You are most able to help her establish relationships, avoid loneliness, and live a fulfilling lifestyle.

WHAT ABOUT YOUR NEEDS?

There is a part of our being that may never want to let go of a child who has needed more care than most. You want to keep her safe from all the dangers of this world. At the same time, you know that it is unlikely you can be there for the rest of her life. If you don't make arrangements that work for her, she will be unprepared for the time when you can't be there for her.

The commitment to your child has been long and strong. You have undoubtedly made sacrifices that many parents haven't had to make. Maybe you've never had vacations, however short, away from your child. Everything had to be adapted to what worked for her care, comfort, and security, so your life has not worked out the way you thought it would. You may have never had time to take care of yourself—and now your body and soul is telling you it is time.

I have heard comments from many parents who feel as though their life has been held captive by care throughout the childhood of their son or daughter. They long for simple freedom to have some life for themselves. There is a conflict between your responsibility to your child, yourself, and your spouse. If only you can find a happy life for your adult child, then maybe the other responsibilities will be reconciled, or so it seems.

The path to transition can be frustrating for your adult child and for you. Things need to be right for her before you'll feel comfortable concentrating on your own needs. And accomplishing that is no slam dunk. It may be hard for you to let go, and it may be hard for her to let go of you.

Maybe your 30-year-old adult daughter has just moved into a group home after a long time on a waiting list. You think she is stable, and all will be well for her forever. You can take the vacations that you have longed for. You have the time to accomplish some of your dreams. The phone calls and meetings about her adjustment are just because it is new to her. She will eventually adjust and have the happy life both of you dreamed of for her. Then you can move on to being an "empty nester." In fact, a year (or even five years) later you may be still thinking the same thing.

BECOMING PROACTIVE

Reality can be a bitter pill to swallow, but hopefully, some of the ideas we will discuss will help reduce it. Let's face some of it together from the start.

If no alternative programs are immediately available upon graduation from high school, and she is not able to function independently at home while you continue your outside employment, this can have a major impact on the family unit as a whole. Plus, it can be boring and anxiety producing for an adult child. Either you'll need to stay at home with her or find staff to come in while you are at work. Sometimes you can get funding from governmental programs, but it still stresses the family unit, especially if staff is hard to find or undependable.

If we wait for services to become available because we are aged or unable to care for our adult children, we will not have the same ability to aid in the transition. The longer an adult child remains in the nest, the more difficult will be her transition to an adult situation.

Raising our children with special needs, we fight schools and constantly deal with medical and other issues. It is likely that the people least taken care of are ourselves. As a result, it is possible that we will experience energy issues and health problems at a younger age than average. In fact, you may find it harder to take care of her today than when you were younger, especially if she is very active, requires lifting, needs assistance with her bath, or experiences behavior problems.

Accepting that the nest is going to be full for longer than anticipated can be paralyzing and fearful. You might not want to accept the reality that you will not be able to take care of her as well as you once did and that her transition needs to begin.

Take steps to prepare her for transition even though opportunities may not be available. It will go a long way toward making transition easier when the time comes. Strong advocacy by you as a parent may help to open doors for her that wouldn't open any other way.

When you are no longer able to be the advocate, advocacy will continue to be important. Self-advocates are more common today than before. You can help your adult child learn to find out details and advocate for her own services and opportunities. If she is not able to become a self-advocate, you may want to locate a family member, friend, or professional who will be ready to advocate for her when you are no longer her primary advocate. By working together now, the path of transition to self-advocacy or another advocate will be smoother, and information will be readily available for that process.

It is possible that together you and your adult child can create an individualized plan while waiting for vocational or residential programs to become available. Maybe some services are available without being in a specific program. For example, if she qualifies for in-home support staff, it is possible that you can have that staff person work with her on community activities at the same time instead of waiting for a vocational program. You may also be able to get her on a waiting list to receive reduced-rate rental housing through your local housing authority.

Whatever the degree of assistance needed, it is vital to plan early and prepare your child for the transition to adulthood as best you can. Hopefully, you are reading this before she is at the stage of actually moving into transition from the nest. If so, it will be easier to create a system that is just right for your child. We can look at what works for her as an individual and prepare her better for transition.

This may seem like a lot to deal with. And it is. There is a peace that comes from feeling that you have prepared your child to have a good life even if you can't keep her in the nest where she was raised. You may never be able to experience the freedom that some empty nesters do, but perhaps you will take pleasure in seeing your child reach her goals. And once the planning is complete, you may be able to relax more.

That having been said, it is not necessary to overdo. Remember that you are redeeming wasted time (that would have been spent waiting for services). Do what you can to plan and adapt the suggestions herein to what works for you and your child. Take what is helpful and leave the rest.

Sometimes it will definitely feel easier to keep her at home with you as long as you can take care of her. That is probably true, and she may even be most happy in the nest where she feels secure. The problem is that when you are no longer able to take care of her, there are no guarantees your plans for her will be understood and carried out. If she waits, it will only be harder for her.

2

THAT NAGGING QUESTION

WHAT HAPPENS TO MY CHILD WHEN I'M GONE?

You know that question so well if you are the parent of a child or adult who experiences special needs. In some ways the question is more difficult to deal with today than it was in past decades when we knew that we couldn't depend on government interventions to the degree we expect today. Friends and family were more comfortable making commitments to be there when we could no longer take care of our loved ones. Now everyone has busier lives, and we are such a mobile society that family members may live so far away they never really get to know your adult child. The situation becomes more complicated. There are some government programs, but never enough to meet the needs of all of today's adults who experience disabilities. Even the closing of the large institutions makes the question more complicated. We may not have wished for placement in an institution, but at least it was a backup plan.

We have all heard horror stories about adults who are not properly cared for or taken advantage of after their parents die. It is scary to think of your adult child being unprotected after your death. Parents often express the hope to survive the child by at least 5 minutes so it won't be a problem. Some have actually taken tragic steps to assure they survive their child.

I can understand that because my own son, Billy Ray, now 26 years old, is very complex. He experiences multiple medical problems, developmental disability, and mental health diagnoses that include behavior problems. To compound these problems, the medical issues are often more the cause of his behavior than the developmental disability diagnosis or mental health diagnoses. It is difficult to find the right residential and vocational program for him. A program that can deal with his behavior may not be equipped to deal with his multiple medical challenges and vice versa.

In a perfect world, you would hire support staff that would remain with your child long after you could not provide direct care. Staff would be trained by you and pass that training on to the next person. According to the former brokerage that managed the government funding for his in-home supports, we generally keep staff for an average of one year. That's longer than the four- to six-month average.

We have tried having in-home staff for Billy Ray. In fact, if you have read my previous book, you know I wrote about how to train and maintain staff. That type of resource is important, but we haven't been able to do that for Billy Ray recently because:

- Finding employees—especially in-home support staff—is difficult in our area.
- Billy Ray's current medical issues require absolute consistency in care and monitoring. We have had much difficulty getting that with anyone but family.
- Billy Ray's aggressive behaviors usually result from medical issues. The response of staff can be fear or aggression; both are a concern.
- Billy Ray bonds to most of his support staff rather quickly. The loss of a staff person who moves on is very traumatic to him. Thus, we have been giving him a break from that trauma until we get him medically stable.

Billy Ray remains at home with his stepfather and me. We plan to have support staff with the idea that eventually Billy Ray will have his own home with staff trained in place to help him maintain the environment he needs to be comfortable and less agitated.

We have Billy Ray's care sort of down to our own science and it works for us. However, at 57 years old with a family history of stroke and other health issues, it is a concern that crosses my mind often. I ask myself, *What if I can't set him up in an adult placement before something happens to me?*

This is even more worrisome because his difficult (sometimes explosive or aggressive) behavior is frequently interpreted as something that can only be treated with medication. I am not against medication, but have learned from my best teacher, Billy Ray, that it is not always the best answer. Billy Ray's explosive or agitated behavior may be related to a physical issue or a change in routine that confuses him.

While the following examples may seem off subject for this chapter, bear with me; it will become clear why they add to that nagging question. Billy Ray has had two incidents where his life could have been strongly impacted by misinterpretation.

Because he describes a horror-filled situation during bath time while in a treatment center as a teenager, he requires absolute consistency in the process of his bath. Once, I methodically trained a new staff person in his bath routine by providing her with instructions complete with pictures and by having her watch me do the routine with him for one full week and then watching her to do the routine with him for another week before allowing her to do it independently with him. The following week she changed part of his routine: It was a simple thing—she helped him put on his T-shirt earlier in the process. He seemed to accept this during the five days each week that she assisted him with his bath. She never mentioned the change in routine to me. And each weekend when I assisted him with his bath, I returned to the original routine. When I would not put his T-shirt on him at the same point in the process that she had been doing it, he became agitated out of confusion. As the weeks went by, he became increasingly aggressive toward me.

Another example was a time when his aggression toward me was reaching dangerous proportions. At the same time, he was also experiencing physical issues. His primary medical provider instructed me to take Billy Ray to the emergency room on a Saturday because he had done all he could to find the cause of Billy Ray's behavior and worsening health. The emergency room doctor stated clearly and repeatedly that there was nothing physically wrong with Billy Ray. He wanted to send him home on psychiatric medication. I strongly advocated that there was something physical occurring and that he was in pain. When they finally did a CAT scan, they discovered that Billy Ray had a leaking appendix, an enlarged pancreas, severe acid reflux, and the beginning of an ulcer. He was rushed into emergency surgery.

Why do these examples add to that nagging question? For one thing, had I agreed to the emergency room doctor's plan to send him home on psychiatric medications for the behavior rather than finding the physical problem, Billy Ray could be dead now. In the bath routine example, the increasing aggression could have caused him to be placed in a facility for aggressive children or adults. It might have resulted in his being given strong enough medication to render him zombie-like had we not researched the cause and dealt with it. Because I understand his "communication by behavior" better than others, I worry more about what will happen to him when I am no longer here to interpret his behavior and try to find solutions.

This chapter was already written on New Year's Eve 2007, the day I experienced major breathing problems and was rushed to the hospital. During the ambulance ride, the EMT kept saying that if I didn't slow my breathing, I wouldn't make it to the hospital. All of the above ran through my mind. Was everything ready so that others would know what Billy Ray needs even if I didn't have everything in place for his transition? What *should* I have done but did not have time to finish? It turned out to be a minor heart attack, not life threatening. But the panic it brought on was a wakeup call for me.

After coming home from the hospital, I requested a meeting with the case manager. He reminded me that when an adult must be placed because his parents can no longer take care of him, the vacancy may not be in the area where he resides. The case manager mentioned the coast, which is approximately 200 miles from Billy Ray's community and his relationships.

Once, when I needed to be away from Billy Ray for a few weeks, this distance problem was dealt with. We wanted him nearby so he could see his friends, attend the school program we had struggled so hard to create, and go to church in as close to his routine as possible. It took strong advocacy and basic refusal to accept anything less. Now the nagging question is, *What happens when I am not there to advocate for him?* Thus, the importance of the next chapter, "Loneliness Is the Only Real Disability." Establishing relationships to prevent loneliness is vital. Establishing relationships with people who will assure contact even if it is not convenient and who you can

trust to stand up and advocate strongly for your adult child is the most important thing you can to do for him.

I learned something else during my recovery that horrified me. Because
of the way my minor heart attack had come on with no warning, I was
nervous about my husband leaving Billy Ray and I alone for extended periods of time. We very much wanted him to be able to attend his daughter's
graduation from college, but that would require Larry to leave Billy Ray
and I for a few days. I talked to a friend about being available to come over
with Billy Ray until the case manager could be reached in the event of an
emergency.

I called the county case manager to ask if I could give our friend his cell
phone number in case of an emergency. Having moved from a metropolitan
area where I knew that there were temporary "crisis beds" in the event of an
emergency, it was my expectation that this would occur until my husband
or I returned. I learned that they have no coverage or crisis homes, etc., on
the weekends. In the event of an emergency, the police would have to be
called, and if Billy Ray had to be placed temporarily, it would be in a regular
nursing home until the office was open, and they could work out some sort
of placement for him.

The reason this was horrifying to me was twofold. First, Billy Ray would
be totally freaked by the appearance of a uniformed officer and ride in the
police car. He and his deceased father used to watch the television program
Cops. Once, a uniformed officer came to the house on what was judged an
unfounded child abuse complaint. Billy Ray thought he was a "bad boy" like
from the theme song of the television program and was sure he was going
to jail. It impacted him for months, even though nothing came of the
complaint. I can only imagine his reaction if he actually had to ride in a police car.

Additionally, I can see that placing him in a nursing home would not
work for either the other residents or Billy Ray. He would be frightened, so
his behavior would intensify including noise and activity. He is not a typical runaway from home, but he did run away from an uncomfortable classroom situation once. I think that is a real risk. He could also become
aggressive if he became afraid.

It is easy to become paralyzed from the fear of that nagging question.
However, it doesn't have to be that way. You can experience the peace of
mind that comes from knowing you have done everything you can to make
the transition smooth.

MAKING PEACE WITH THAT NAGGING QUESTION

There are so many unknowns, not only in your child's future but in your own as well. Fear of the unknown is very difficult to live with. There are many things you can do make sure your adult child gets the level of support he needs and that allows him to live a life that is fulfilling to him. As you arrive at the conclusion that you have done everything possible to document your knowledge of your child and help him to establish a quality adult life, you will feel much more at peace.

An adult who experiences disabilities and is able to live independently may still require followup by parents or part-time staff. Whether verbal or not, he may have difficulty communicating what he needs verbally. Programs that offer support come and go—as does the staff they employ. You wonder whether anyone will follow up on your son or daughter if you can't do it personally. Having the documentation and planning spelled out (as we will discuss in Chapter 11, "Implementing the Plan a Step at a Time") will allow your training methods and involvement to survive your ability to be there personally.

Assisting an adult child to find a fulfilling life is more complicated when he experiences disabilities, but it can be done. The same pride of watching an adult child enjoy life is achievable if you adapt to what works for him and what he enjoys.

Even the most difficult issues can probably be adapted in some way to deal with the problem. For example, the horror I mentioned that Billy Ray might be moved away from the community relationships we have struggled to create might be dealt with by establishing his own home and setting up supports sooner. If that isn't achievable immediately, there could be a backup family who would agree to become specially certified foster parents in the event I am not available to him and until more permanent arrangements can be made. (See Appendix A for the Sample Emergency Backup Plan and Appendix B for the Sample Caregiver's Manual I have prepared to deal with that potential situation.) At the very least, family and/or friends can be taught to be advocates for him.

While waiting on service waiting lists, you can begin helping him discover what he wants in his life as an adult. You can try to get some training and/or provide other training at home toward both vocational and residential situations. You may even be able to create a life that is much less dependent on governmental agencies than you had expected.

As stated, it is best if your adult child is actually transitioned while you can still be a strong advocate for him. However, by doing the preliminary planning with and for him, having relationships in place with people who will advocate for him and documentation available, transition without your help will be further ahead than it might otherwise be. That nagging question is conquered—or at least quieted—by the preparation and planning we will discuss in subsequent chapters. There is more peace when we see that things are in place for the kind of life that makes our adult child as happy as possible.

There are some hard realities in dealing with nagging questions—including some you may not want to face. For example, Billy Ray's case manager is always reminding me that it is unlikely anyone will have the same commitment to Billy Ray that I do, no matter how noble his or her intentions. However, showing those who will advocate for him the principles of team-building advocacy, as opposed to the principles of combat-fighting advocacy, will increase the likelihood of their success. Helping them to understand what is important to your adult child and why certain things happen assures a greater understanding and commitment to your child than there might otherwise have been.

There may be things that will occur after you are not involved that you could not possibly have anticipated. Unfortunately, some of that is unavoidable. But there is also peace in accepting that you have done what you could.

Suppose you plan for your child to inherit the family home and have staff come in to provide whatever level of assistance he requires. Maybe you even hired staff and trained them while you are able to participate in the training. A few months or a year after the training has been in place you may think you have it all arranged. Then the staff leaves, and you get to start all over again. You may find it hard to keep good staff. You worry about what happens when you are not able to keep taking care of him. Starting over again will, of course, be frustrating, but you will do it because of your commitment to your child.

As we will discuss in the next chapter, building relationships between your child and others will bring you even more peace. These relationships may not be with future caregivers, but if they stay involved with him, there is a greater chance of maintaining the life your adult child and you envision.

TRANSITION PLANNING EASES THAT NAGGING QUESTION

I recommend starting transition planning at about age 10 to 12. That is ideal because you can get necessary skills included in the IEP as goals for training. Of course, you may not have the luxury of time. Wherever he is, you can begin to set goals and make plans.

Parents are best able to work with their children to determine an effective transition plan. Yes, professionals will play an important role. But parental involvement makes things more secure for the adult child, and it adds to the chance of a successful transition.

Probably the hardest part of transition planning is that, to some degree, you are preparing for your replacement. It is much more emotional than training your replacement before retiring from a long career. It will also take a lot more people to accomplish it.

You have likely been your child's best friend, advocate, financial manager, caregiver, and more. And now you will need to assure that either he is trained to do those things for himself or that others are trained to meet his needs. It is hard to imagine someone else doing things for him that you have always done and hard to recognize that perhaps he can do some of it himself. At the same time, you recognize that you will not likely be able to do those things forever.

As you will see in the following chapters, there are many things you can do to help with the transition. You will be able to help ascertain what he wishes for his adult life. As his parent, you know him best and will be his most powerful advocate.

As you work through transition planning, the pressure of that nagging question will subside—but only to a degree. Realistically, the question is never far from our hearts. But again, there is peace in knowing that you have done everything you could do to assure a happy and secure life for him when you can't be there to provide it.

3

LONELINESS IS THE ONLY REAL DISABILITY

RELATIONSHIPS—THE MOST IMPORTANT PART OF LIFE

I first heard the phrase "Loneliness is the only real disability" used in a presentation by Dr. David Pitonyak at a conference where we were both speaking. Apparently David and others had borrowed it from Dr. Beth Mount, who has allowed me to use it here. It says so much about the importance of relationships in our lives.

The sense of being alone is scary. It evokes different emotions for each of us. Some may be withdrawn. Others will be angry and demonstrate undesirable behavior. We can cope with our fears and frustrations over many other issues so much easier when there is someone to share them with. Sharing our joys makes them even better. Feeling alone can be truly disabling.

If you think about it, chances are you know someone who is so lonely and unhappy that she seems stuck, even if she has no disability. She doesn't necessarily admit she is lonely, even though she is capable of communicating it. That's because it is embarrassing. People who have disabilities but also have good friends and family can be happier despite any challenges they may experience in everyday life.

As parents, we worry about financial arrangements, medical care, and appropriate housing for adult children with special needs. Some of the important issues may not be obvious. While we are actively involved in her life, whether she is still at home in the nest, we visit her in her own apartment or care home each week, or talk to her on the phone daily, loneliness may not seem to be a problem. Maybe you take her out to lunch on a certain day each week, or she comes to your home for the weekend. She has something to look forward to and count on. She is happy when you are together, so loneliness is not so evident. She can cook her breakfast, take her medications on time, and do housework with the help of an independent living trainer. But does she understand how to maintain the relationships that are important to her? This skill, to the degree she is able to achieve it, will do more to enhance her life than having the best job or the most beautiful apartment.

Imagine being forced to work in a sheltered workshop doing work you may not enjoy, living in a group home where the residents come and go (and some may be major irritants to your serenity). Staff goes home after every shift, and frequently they never come back. Even if you are verbal, no one seems to know your history. They don't know what you did when you lived with your parents. They don't know who your grandparents were.

Sometimes even a service dog (which is granted as an accommodation under the ADA) would help greatly with the loneliness but is not allowed to go residential programs with the person. Billy Ray experienced that twice. The first one was a residential treatment center where he was placed for the purpose of changing his medication. The administration feared Billy Ray's service dog would set off other residents or that the dog might be harmed. The second time was when we placed Billy Ray in a specialized adult foster home because I was unable to care for him for several weeks. The county case manager told me that if the foster home was unwilling to take the dog, we would not be able to force them into it. Provider after provider rejected the dog. All my attempts to advocate by citing the ADA failed. I asked how one government office could refuse to comply with ADA and was told they were not refusing to allow Billy Ray to have the service dog. But if I pushed, they would refuse to place Billy Ray because they didn't have a placement that would accept the dog. Even the companionship of Billy Ray's service dog, which would have kept him calmer and helped with the loneliness of being away from his family, was denied.

Several years ago I was privileged to attend a few sessions led by Dr. David Pitonyak at a conference where we were both speaking. David has a way of making his points stick by using humor to drive them home. For example, he asked how we would feel if everyone who spent time with us was paid to do so. Dr. Pitonyak writes on his website (www.dimagine.com): "Although paid staff can be friendly and supportive, they frequently change jobs or take on new responsibilities. The resulting instability can be devastating to someone who is fundamentally alone."

Your adult child will undoubtedly bond to skills trainers who come into her place of residence to help with various tasks. Yet, job turnover is often months, not years. If there are no outside relationships such as family and friends to comfort her through that loss, it can be devastating.

Relationships with paid staff can be very different from relationships with friends who really know you as a person, for whom it's not a job and who care about you for who you are. Dr. Pitonyak gave an illustration in one of the presentations: "I often ask people to imagine what it would be like if I arrived home from one of my business trips and, instead of finding my lovely wife Cyndi, there was another woman. I would ask 'Where's Cyndi?' And imagine how I would feel if she said, 'Cyndi's not home. But don't worry. We have you covered!' " (personal communication). In his trademark, humorous style, Dr. Pitonyak gently pointed out: "Caring *about* someone is not the same thing as taking care *of* someone."

I believe there are many paid staff who genuinely care about those to whom they provide care. It becomes more than just a job to many. Some will stay in a low-paid job for years because they love their work and the people they work with.

It helps to think about what you might discuss with a friend you have known since elementary school versus a new co-worker with whom you have become friendly. If you don't get together often with a longtime friend, chances are you spend most of your time together remembering old times. Generally, you really know each other as individuals and relate better than you do to someone you have not known long. Clearly, that kind of relationship is more meaningful than one with a paid staffer who will only be with you six months to a year and then move on. The time to build that special bond of friendship is missing. Also missing is each other's history.

Your childhood friend knows about that ugly dog that you loved so much, the boy you had a crush on in high school, who your parents and grandparents were, and how many siblings you had. But when you interact with short-term staff members, these important parts of knowing you are missing.

Some persons who experience special needs have difficulty forming relationships outside of the family. Often their relationships are with family friends more than with individual friends. The friendship functions in the context of the family home, but it may not be strong enough to endure after leaving the home. She may need some help in forming and maintaining those types of relationships to enable them to continue into her transition.

After the death of Billy Ray's dad, I married Larry, who is the father of four adult children and grandfather of twelve grandchildren. Billy Ray loves being "Uncle Billy Ray." I have noticed that each of his "neeceys" and "nefews" respond to him differently. Some have made a genuine effort to get to know him; they obviously care about Billy Ray.

While most of the grandkids love Billy Ray and are gentle with him, some relationships are particularly special to watch. One is a teenager who, even as a young girl, had a special bond with Billy Ray. When we would be talking on the phone and she would hear Billy Ray's agitated-sounding noise in the background, she would ask, "Is that Uncle Billy Ray?" When I would respond that it was, she would say, "Let me talk to him, it will help." And it never failed to calm him for a while. To this day he talks to her on the phone longer than he will to anyone else. While he loves doing activities with all his nieces and nephews, it just seems to flow better with her. She is able to understand him better, and vice versa. It is a special relationship for both of them.

She is still young, and I wouldn't put pressure on her at this stage. But I do make it a point to tell her stories about when Billy Ray was a baby. I share with her who he is. She loves this and it helps her to understand him better. I actually do the same with others too, but it appears more meaningful with this particular "neecey." It is my hope that he will be able to have a relationship with his nieces and nephews long after Larry and I are gone.

If you notice those types of special relationships with family members or friends, help her to preserve them. You may have to structure it for her. For example, make a note on the calendar or planner to telephone her special person regularly; send cards for the person's birthday, Christmas, and other holidays; and if feasible, invite her special person to visit as often as possible.

Relationships can develop from common interests. If she loves bowling, take her bowling or arrange for her to go bowling whenever possible. People get used to seeing her there, and sometimes they begin to speak to each other. If there is a spark of friendship, help her to cultivate it by having a soda together at the bowling alley, inviting the new friend to visit her in her home, planning bowling dates, or doing some other activity they might enjoy together.

If church relationships were established while she was still in the nest, make it a point to encourage them as she transitions to adult living arrangements. Assure that she will always be able to attend her church if she wishes. If she loves the church potlucks, help her write that into her adult life so she can continue to do what she enjoys.

While Billy Ray has many friends at our little church, one couple in particular are very involved in his life. Donna often makes the high-fiber cookies for him that he needs because he will eat hers better than Mom's (even though they are both made from the same recipe). Her husband, Max, plays the piano at church. Billy Ray loves his music and his hugs.

On the refrigerator is a picture of Billy Ray blowing out the candles on Donna's birthday cake. He loves that picture. He has another copy of it that he carries around with him often. Every morning and throughout the day he stands at the refrigerator and greets his Donna. Although they are "snowbirds" and spend winter away from our little town, Donna and Max are always thinking of Billy Ray when they are away. For example, they know he loves John Wayne movies, so they might send him a movie or some John Wayne trinket. Once they had a T-shirt made for him with John Wayne on it and sent it to him while they were out of town.

When Billy Ray misses Donna, he can call her and talk to her on the cell phone. It never fails to perk him up even if he isn't feeling well. Additionally, this is great social training for him.

Billy Ray lost some of his social skills during two health crises. But I have noticed that because of the relationship he has with Donna and Max, he is regaining those skills. For example, he used to call special friends and family to sing "Happy Birthday" when someone had a birthday. For a while after his health crises he was willing to call but he wouldn't really talk, let alone sing. Now that he is talking and singing to Donna and Max, he is talking more and singing "Happy Birthday," when appropriate, to others.

TEACHING HER TO MAINTAIN RELATIONSHIPS

As relationships are established, enter related communication on her schedule in whatever way she can accomplish it. If she is verbal, note that she should call the friend at a certain frequency that seems appropriate, or that she should invite her friend(s) to do some activity together. Or they could have regular times to bowl or do activities they both enjoy.

Have some sort of a telephone directory available to her (and keep a backup copy). If she is nonverbal create a picture list of her friends and family and put them in a small notebook with the address and phone number for each person near his or her photo. That way she can indicate to you or to support staff when she wants to see the person or wants to write a note to them.

It is hard to put yourself in your adult child's position after your death. Grief may be expressed differently than for those without disabilities. Billy Ray's dad died when he was 11 years old. It was very difficult for him to accept that Daddy wasn't coming back or that we couldn't immediately go out and get a new daddy. This was a constant topic of conversation for a long time. It reduced later when he got a stepfather, but he still talks about his dad frequently. He also seems to have a sense of time near the anniversary of his dad's death and birthday. During those times he speaks of his father many times a day even now, fourteen years after his death.

I remember discussing Billy Ray's grief with his psychiatrist. He said that most people think of lost loved ones frequently, but just stop talking about them. Billy Ray, however, is not able to get beyond it and stop talking about his dad.

The pain of grief lasts for years especially if there are triggers to remind you. That has been my experience relative to my maternal grandmother. As a child, I was always in the kitchen helping "Grandma" while my cousins were occupied with one another. Grandma taught me how to bake. Holiday meals at Grandma's were always special. Even though she died twenty years ago, I miss those special times. It is worse when I am not actively involved in a special gathering.

Prepare your adult child for that. If she lives independently, it will be particularly lonely if she doesn't have a place to spend holidays or other special times. If there are special friends from her church or other organizations she is involved with, try to have special times together with those friends while you are able to participate, so that they get a chance to observe how she needs things to be for her comfort level. Talk to them about including her in their holidays or spending time with her before or after their family gatherings if that isn't convenient. Don't leave it to chance. In fact, help her to establish relationships with other families too, so that she will always have a surrogate family for special events.

Unfortunately, you may have to be specific about what she needs in order for relationships to work. People who care about her may be unsure of how to respond to some things. Teach her friends how to relate to her just as you teach her how to maintain her friendships with them. For example, if she has behavior issues or care needs, they may be willing to have her visit their home but are unsure of their ability to care for her. Assure them that they can invite her support staff to accompany her. Many times, having the support staff come for just the first few visits is enough, and they won't be needed after that. Suggest that if it is more comfortable, the friends could come to her home rather than the other way around.

It may be hard to anticipate her reaction to loss, but to the degree possible, planning a specific person or activity that will be available to help her deal with losing you when the time comes will make things much easier for her. You might want to make videos of you and her doing things together that will be available to her in the future, or write a letter that can be read to her when she is ready to hear it.

Relationships that will last beyond your ability to stay involved with your adult child are vital to reduce loneliness. They also add a degree of protection to those who don't have active involvement by their own family members. It is a sad fact that abuse happens, and persons who experience disabilities are more vulnerable. When friends or families are actively involved in their lives, it decreases the risk. It is beneficial to establish these relationships while a parent can be involved to help cultivate them.

YOUR ADULT CHILD'S STORY

Much of who we are as persons comes from our families and our life experiences. We love to share those memories with friends and family. That is more difficult for people with special needs who have lost contact with their families. And it is especially challenging if an adult is nonverbal or only partly verbal.

Having her own story in a book or album will be a comfort to her. She will be able to share who she is with the people in her life and reflect on people from the past. In addition to the memories and sense of knowing or being known, the story helps professionals understand personal preferences and abilities; it aids in understanding her as a person. It adds dimension and invites respect.

WRITING YOUR CHILD'S STORY

As you may know from my earlier writings or speaking, my most important concept is *adapt and communicate*. That applies to writing the story of your child's life. A system that works for her is key to its future value. It needs to work for her so that she can enjoy not only looking at it, but also sharing it with significant others in her life. The time spent adapting it to her use and creating it will bring her untold hours of joy and comfort over the years.

Some agencies provide fill-in-the-blanks forms to document a child's story and some tools to help write the story are available commercially. You can also create your own format. In determining what works best for her, think about how she enjoys photo albums or other books now. The following are some things to consider:

- Is she articulate enough to share verbally with others based on a picture cue alone?
- Is she able to read a written story with some pictures?
- Is it something that she will enjoy having read to her frequently?
- Will she enjoy it more if it is shorter or divided into two or three smaller volumes?
- What kind of binder cover will last longest and be easy for her to hold and view?

I started telling Billy Ray the story of his adoption when he was very small. I read that you should tell small children their adoption stories just as you would tell any other story. When I started making visuals for him, I put the story of his adoption into the visuals we call his stories. (You can see a sample of his adoption story on my website at www.parentingyourcomplexchild.com/AdoptionStory.html.) They are printed on photo paper to make them heavier and clearer (he has low vision) then laminated and put in three-ring binders. This is the best format for him. He loves his stories. Sometimes he just likes to look at them alone, and sometimes he will bring them to me to read to him. Other times he will bring them to guests and want them to read to him. In that way he is sharing who he is with others. The stories are so well read that they need to be reprinted occasionally because they fall apart from use. I have them on computer disk and reprint and laminate as often as he needs it. Sometimes it is only necessary to reprint a few pages; sometimes the whole notebook.

If your child is high functioning, a nice picture album with small captions of who is pictured might be adequate. Captions need not be as detailed for some, but we all need triggers for our memory. If you add the role of the person pictured, it might help staff and professionals to understand how meaningful the relationship is.

If you are using a photo album as opposed to doing story visuals, and she would have difficulty communicating who or what is in the picture, you can add more detailed captions or number each picture to correspond with a paragraph in the back of the album (or instead of numbering you could put a thumbnail of the picture next to the paragraph in the back). This will help significant others understand more about her life and relationships after you're gone.

This Christmas we bought Billy Ray one of those digital picture frames that holds lots of digital pictures and displays them as a slideshow. He loves it and stops to watch for several minutes at a time throughout the day. You would still want to have some kind of written description if your child would not be able to tell others who is pictured and what their role in her life is. Since it displays the pictures in random order, you may want to print a thumbnail of each picture next to the description.

I am not sure how durable the digital frame will be. If your child lives in a facility, it is probably also vulnerable to other residents. It is probably a good idea to have it as an addition to some kind of printed album or visual notebook. Another option would be to have someone maintain a disk with all the pictures on it, so a new one could be reloaded with the same pictures if the initial one is lost or broken.

Whatever format you choose, include various periods of her life such as the following:

- Baby and childhood pictures. If you do it in a story rather than an album, include stories about what was going on when she was born, who her parents, grandparents, and siblings are, and any other pertinent items.
- Family pictures and stories at various stages in her life; include family holidays or meaningful vacations.
- School and special activity pictures:
  - Various school pictures and stories, although maybe not every year to keep her story from becoming too long.
  - Little League, scouting, or other favorite activities.
  - Camp and other special activities/places.

WHO WILL MAINTAIN THE STORY?

I have thought of this question for Billy Ray a lot. I don't expect his niece (mentioned earlier) to actually become Billy Ray's caregiver someday. However, because they already share his stories (from the visuals), I hope that she will maintain contact with him and continue to share his story with him.

Times and people change. Family and friends move away or become occupied in other areas of their lives. Contact deteriorates. Thus, having more than one person aware of your child's story is desirable.

And it's vital to have more than one copy of the album or the printed stories. People move, things get lost, floods and fires happen. Perhaps a copy of her story can be in her home and one in your home with instructions to have it provided to some specific person upon your death. The other option is to put a second copy on a CD and in your planning file or another specified place where others can find it. Attach a note to the CD with any special preparation tips (for example, if story pages are laminated, they will last longer).

Helping her to establish relationships with friends and family and keep her identity by maintaining her story may be one of the most important things you can do in transition planning. The joy and comfort it brings will help her deal with the disappointments that we all experience in life.

As Dr. Beth Mount shared with me, she could present two sides to the story because of her role as the sibling of a person with disabilities. She has become the person she is today as the result of having her brother in her life. Her life's work and passion was inspired by that relationship. On the other hand, her family life was significantly impacted. Her family sacrificed and faced challenges because of her brother.

Many parents naturally expect that adult children without disabilities will take care of a child with disabilities. There is a strong likelihood that siblings have been taking care of a disabled brother or sister to some degree throughout their childhood. If caregivers do more of the actual care and allow siblings to advocate, visit, and to do things together as adult siblings normally do, it may become an even more meaningful adult relationship.

FRIENDS AS ADVOCATES

Family and friends who really know your adult child as a person are the absolute best advocates. As a result of Donna and Max's friendship with Billy Ray, they would be great advocates. Donna has a strong desire to understand what works for Billy Ray and anticipate his reaction to events, gifts, or other issues. She frequently asks questions that help her to understand Billy Ray better. At times I also explain his reactions to help her know him as he is. Donna knows him better than anyone not actually living in the house because she cares enough to learn who he is.

Donna and Max would probably not be the primary advocates for Billy Ray because they are snowbirds and travel most of the winter months. However, it is a great comfort to know that if something should happen to me, Donna would be able to clarify many things about Billy Ray.

I can picture Donna calling the county case management people and getting others to call too if they placed Billy Ray in a distant city away from his friends and community relationships.

Some relationships are not formed as naturally as the relationship between Billy Ray and Donna. It may well take some effort on your part to help others know your adult child as a person, but it is well worth the effort.

As she forms relationships, observe anyone who shows commitment to her. Talk to her friends about whether they would consider having a role in her life after you are no longer available. At the very beginning, make sure to clarify that you are talking about being a friend and advocate, not about moving in. People who are unsure how to care for someone who experiences disabilities often panic at the thought; this reassurance may make a difference in someone's willingness to participate.

When possible, invite the friend to accompany you to team meetings. Help the friend-advocate to see the difference between fighting for your child and team-building advocacy. Explain that being overly assertive doesn't accomplish the desired goals.

In determining relationships that will ease the loneliness your adult child may experience, think about her as a person. Will she want lots of company, or is she a person who likes a little companionship but still wants a fair degree of personal space? What kinds of things would family and friends be most helpful for? What relationships does she have now that might stop if you were not there to keep them going?

After determining what relationships will be important for your child in the future, step back and think of them from the family's or friend's position. For example, Donna, who is probably Billy Ray's best friend, is probably not going to be comfortable assisting him with toileting and dressing. On the other hand, I have talked with another friend from our church who had sons and took care of an elderly family member in their home. She would not be bothered by helping with toileting if that would be required when Billy Ray was at church or some social event. Thus, it will be important to ascertain the comfort level of the friend you ask to be involved in your child's adult life. If you don't explain the role to the friend, unknown, uncomfortable things may occur, and willingness to be involved later may change.

The goal of building relationships is to help your adult child feel that she belongs to a circle of friends or family who care about her, know her as she is, and are there for her.

4

Your Child's Pursuit of Happiness

THE STRUGGLE FOR RIGHTS

> We hold these truths to be self evident: that all men are created equal; that they are endowed by their Creator with certain inalienable rights; that among these are life, liberty, and the pursuit of happiness; that to secure these rights, governments are instituted among men, deriving their just powers from the consent of the governed; that whenever any form of government becomes destructive to the ends, it is the right of the people to alter or abolish it, and to institute new government, laying its foundation on such principles, and organizing its powers in such form, as to them shall seem most likely to effect their safety and happiness.[6]

Mr. Jefferson included nothing about basing equality and rights on an individual's level of functioning or intelligence. He held the government responsible for providing it to the governed. In the absence of that, the government, he wrote, could be changed.

In fact, Thomas Jefferson also said:

In America, no other distinction between man and man had ever been known but that of persons in office exercising powers by authority of the laws, and private individuals. Among these last, the poorest laborer stood on equal ground with the wealthiest millionaire, and generally on a more favored one whenever their rights seem to jar.[7]

Our special needs children and adults have the same right to the pursuit of happiness as everyone else. Following that pursuit will likely be a major uphill climb. Many have tried to establish equal rights for people with disabilities, yet the struggle continues. Small victories are achieved but larger hurdles always seem to emerge.

The pursuit of happiness is more complicated to achieve. Indeed, even the description of what true happiness looks like differs widely among people. Nevertheless, I strongly believe that my son and others who experience disabilities have the right to their own pursuit of happiness.

We hear a lot about the American Dream. Depending on whom you ask, it may include a college education, a successful career of some type, a home of our own, and a family. Some dream of owning their own business or having lots of money. I can't ever remember hearing anyone talk about the American Dream for a person with disabilities. The idea that people with disabilities have something to contribute to society or that they have the right to pursue the American Dream sounds like a foreign concept to many members of our society. If there is any acknowledgment of rights, it is generally no more than humane care with little opportunity to be a contributing member of society. Adults with disabilities deserve a dream, too.

The U.S. government has made some important strides by providing civil protections for people with disabilities (perhaps most notably the Americans with Disabilities Act of 1990) and enacting disability benefits such as SSI, but in their own tradition of creating red tape with every advance, they have made life more complicated (and in many ways worse) than before they added benefits and legislation.

MORE THAN A U.S. PROBLEM

The United States is not the only country that has difficulty providing adequate services. The National Autistic Society in England did a survey through a program they called Think Differently About Autism. According to its website, www.autism.org.uk, it found that:

- 63% of adults with autism do not have enough support to meet their needs.

- 60% of parents say that a lack of support has resulted in their son or daughter having higher support needs in the long term.

- A third of adults (33%) say they have experienced severe mental health difficulties because of a lack of support.

- Over 60% of adults with Asperger's syndrome or high-functioning autism have struggled to receive support from their local authority and/or health service. Of these, 52% were told that they do not fit easily into mental health or learning disability services.

- 61% of adults rely on their families for financial support and 40% live at home with their parents.

- 92% of parents are worried about their children's future when they are no longer able to support them.

You can read their report at www.think-differently.org.uk. The contact information for this organization is found in Appendix F.

The website Disability Rights in Canada: A Virtual Museum (http://disabilityrights.freeculture.ca/index.php) includes a history of the struggle for disability rights in Canada. It is a fascinating story about how hard people with disabilities and others advocated beginning in the 1970s, finally getting legislation passed in the 1980s. Nevertheless, the struggle to survive continues for some in Canada.

Mike Huckabee, one of the candidates originally in the 2008 U.S. Presidential race, mentioned in a televised debate that we are all endowed by our Creator with the right to the pursuit of happiness. However, he added that we are not guaranteed happiness. That statement piqued my interest. It reminded me of my uncle telling me as a child that the only thing we are guaranteed is the opportunity to try to make something of ourselves.

Certainly, I have not gotten every job I wanted or gotten into every educational program to which I applied. There are disappointments along the way for all of us. However, even the pursuit of happiness is more limited for people who experience disabilities.

RED TAPE, CONFUSION, AND A POVERTY TRACK

Things that might be considered rights are effectively withheld by red tape and policies. The Social Security Administration regulations do not specifically prohibit the marriage of a person with disabilities. However, the regulations effectively do that by making it very difficult for many married people who experience disabilities. Depending on whether he receives SSDI or SSI and whom he wants to marry, your son may lose all or part of his benefits if he marries. In effect, the government tells him whom he can marry through an SSDI policy that says a "Disabled Adult Child" will lose all his benefits unless he marries another "Disabled Adult Child."

If a person uses a wheelchair to get around or has limitations of some sort, he may need special accommodations. But he probably dreams of using his abilities and focusing less on his disabilities. The dream might lead to work, his own home, or whatever is important to him.

The U.S. government has made some attempts to provide for equal rights in employment and equal access to public places. The ADA introduced protections and rights to accommodations. At the same time, the government has too many policies that make the pursuit of happiness difficult to achieve. The ADA may be another example of trying to make things better but making them worse instead.

According to David C. Stapleton and Richard V. Burkhauser:

> We would expect that the declining unemployment rates during the growth years of the 1990s business cycle would have caused employers to look beyond their traditional workforce to the millions of working-aged people with disabilities. Yet . . . the overall employment rates of those with disabilities declined during this period. Some argue that the ADA [Americans with Disabilities Act] impeded this process. The ADA, passed in 1990 and effective in 1992, was intended, among other things, to increase the employment of people with disabilities by requiring firms to make reasonable accommodations for "qualified" employees and by banning discrimination against people with disabilities in hiring, firing and pay. Proponents claimed the ADA would induce companies to make adjustments necessary to employ workers with disabilities, and would reduce unlawful discrimination. Critics argued that unintended consequence of increased costs of accommodation and the increased threat of litigation resulting from the act would be a decline in the employment of the very people the ADA was meant to protect.[8]

SSI and SSDI remove incentives to work, according to Andrew Houtenville, PhD, of Cornell University's Rehabilitation Research and Training Center on Disability Demographics and Statistics ("StatsRRTC").[9]

Unless a person with disabilities can get a job with sufficient health insurance and needs little or no governmental assistance, he can become stuck in what David Stapleton refers to as the "poverty trap."[10] Many services are connected to eligibility for SSI or SSDI. Should a disabled person be able to work enough to disqualify him from eligibility for those programs, he may also lose Medicare or state health programs. Working might generate more money, but the state medical card and/or Medicare that provides necessary medication and medical treatment may be worth much more than the SSI cash benefit.

Survival becomes a serious issue without some of those services. On the other hand, that survival generally means poverty because the benefits are so low. SSI runs in the range of $600 per month, which doesn't really provide a decent place to live plus food, clothing, and other necessary expenses. This is what Dr. Stapleton calls the "poverty trap."

The StatsRRTC does an annual Disability Status Report. According to the 2006 Report:

> In 2006, the overall percentage (prevalence rate) of working-age people with a disability ages 21 to 64 in the U.S. was 12.9 percent.
>   In other words, in 2006, 22,382,000 of the 172,961,000 working-age individuals in the U.S. reported one or more disabilities.[11]

The same report shows:

> In 2006, the employment rate of working-age people with disabilities in the U.S. was 37.7 percent.
>   In 2006, the employment rate of working-age people without disabilities was 79.7 percent.
>   The gap between the employment rates of working-age people with and without disabilities was 42.0 percentage points.[12]

The incentive is *not* to use one's abilities, however limited, and remain in poverty just to survive. You can see this by the small percentage of people experiencing disabilities who are employed.

Regarding the rights of persons with disabilities, the government is clearly broken and needs to be changed. There are some steps in that direction, but they are slow and seem to add more confusion and red tape. Thus, parental involvement may be more necessary and more frustrating than during school-age years.

WHY IT IS SO HARD TO GET HELP

Part of the problem in helping your child obtain what will make him happy is the very low expectations many people have for anyone with disabilities. Some people will be nice to children and adults who experience disabilities, but have extremely low expectations of them. As a result, there is resistance to commit resources enabling people living with disabilities to pursue opportunities. Others see them as a drain on the taxpayers and are intolerant. In both situations there is little or no recognition of a person's right to the pursuit of happiness.

Large sheltered workshops that can "serve" many people at once are cheaper to maintain. Individualized jobs that might require job coaches, other training, working with job site personnel to co-ordinate the job experience, and specialized transportation require substantially more funds and effort per person. Faced with budget crunches, doing things on the cheap always seems to supersede respecting individual rights.

In recent years even special education services are being protested as too expensive, especially if they require costly individualized programs because the student doesn't fit in traditional special-education classrooms. The sense that children or adults don't deserve any special services because they are not capable of becoming contributing members of society is communicated in various ways. Some are willing to accept only the bare minimum of humane care—just enough to satisfy our responsibility as taxpayers.

I believe this is at least partly because society as a whole has never been given the opportunity to get to know and understand people with disabilities. They were isolated in institutions or at home until the recent past.

In 1994, Joseph P. Shapiro wrote *No Pity: People with Disabilities Forging a New Civil Rights Movement.*[13] Certainly, a civil rights movement is needed to bring about change, but it seems not to have progressed much since the publication of Mr. Shapiro's wonderful book. Many have tried to bring about change.

In my personal opinion, there are many factors involved in the inability to bring about a lasting change. One is the many conflicting opinions about what is needed. For example, there are those who advocate for research and a cure for autism. There are parents who believe in "the diet" as a legitimate autism treatment, and those who don't. There is much controversy about what is true and which studies are valid and helpful. The conflict among the various factions seems to get in the way of uniting to advocate for change.

Certainly research toward finding a cure for autism and other disabilities is desirable. However, it may not happen fast enough to impact the lives of many children and adults who are alive today. Research should, of course, be funded and pursued to the fullest extent possible. However, it is equally important to advocate for quality lives and opportunities today for those experiencing disabilities now.

The media has been reluctant to cover stories about disabilities. According to writer and editor Susan M. LoTempio in her article "Enabling Coverage of Disabilities," on the Poynter Institute website (www.poynter .org), part of that is because:

> One in five Americans has a disability, according to the last census. That number may mushroom, as baby boomers hit their 60s and face the life-changing health challenges that come with aging.
>
> Still, most reporters shy away from writing stories about disability. They think they're too hard to do. Reporters worry they'll say something during an interview that might offend a person who appears fragile. They worry about getting the jargon and medical terminology right.
>
> Many editors don't assign stories about disability because they're "downers"—the opposite of "inspirational" stories, which are perceived as good news.[14]

Joseph Shapiro describes the problem well:

> Never has the world of disabled people changed so fast. Rapid advances in technology, new civil rights protections, a generation of better-educated disabled students out of "mainstreamed" classrooms, a new group consciousness, and political activism mean more disabled people are seeking jobs and greater daily participation in American

life. But prejudice, society's low expectations, and an antiquated welfare and social service system frustrate these burgeoning attempts at independence. As a result, the new aspirations of people with disabilities have gone unnoticed and misunderstood by mainstream America.[15]

I recently saw someone special to me change her opinion after the media provided her insight. Years ago she felt that too much was being spent on special education, and that it affected property taxes. Last week she shared with me that she had watched coverage on ABC News of a young girl with autism. Apparently, the girl communicated her feelings (using a computer-simulated voice) about how she is treated by the public, and she demonstrated how bright she was. My special person was impressed and said that now she sees people with autism differently because of that media coverage.

Little by little we are getting more glimpses as the media slowly begins to profile people who struggle with their challenges to succeed in one way or another. However, glimpses are still too few to make a significant difference in public response. Unfortunately, fourteen years after Mr. Shapiro's book was published, the aspirations of people with disabilities are still going substantially unnoticed and remain misunderstood.

The documentary *Autism Is a World*, originally aired on CNN, now available on DVD, is about Sue Rubin, who experiences autism. Sue is considered low functioning and at one point was considered to be mentally retarded. However, after she began using facilitative communication, it was discovered that she is highly intelligent.

As of this writing, Sue is 29 years old and lives in her own home. She is able to get funding for 24-hour in-home support staff because she is not able to keep herself safe without it. Her in-home staff accompanies Sue to college courses and assists her with speaking engagements (using facilitative communication).

Sue is quite intelligent. However, total independence might be as unobtainable to her as it would be to someone considered substantially lower functioning. By using services to keep her safe, she is able to create a life that is as fulfilling as possible. She has become a great advocate for others who experience disabilities—offering powerful, encouraging messages.

If society hasn't been allowed to get acquainted with someone, his mannerisms, speech (or lack thereof), and various noises he might make can be scary. It may appear that he is incapable of doing any meaningful activities.

As people with disabilities are profiled in the media or become known in the community, acceptance will become greater and the pursuit of happiness should become easier.

While the struggle for jobs and training continues, it is important to note that we are making slow progress in terms of more accessibility. And more people with disabilities are being seen in the community. There is a long way to go, but it is moving in the right direction.

In the meantime, welcome to the struggle to get appropriate opportunities for a single adult child. You may have thought when he graduated from high school you were done with the tumultuous IEP meetings where you likely had to fight "the team" for educational goals to be added to the plan. Now you will likely have an ISP (Individual Service Plan) team to meet with. Programs and governmental agencies often have teams just like you dealt with in school. Just as when he was in school, your perception of what he can do may not be demonstrated to the team members by his daily response to his present environment. This creates additional hurdles to climb in the struggle for appropriate services.

In *Parenting Your Complex Child*, I shared part of our experience in getting school professionals to see what Billy Ray could do:

> It was difficult for medical, educational, and social-work professionals to believe my claims of what Billy Ray could do. The Billy Ray they saw threw himself on the floor, refused to sit in his chair for table activities, and created havoc in many settings. Thus, when I said, "If only we could figure out how to bring this motivation to control his behavior [when he fed the horse at home] into the rest of his life, he'd be happier and need less medication," the professionals could not picture what I was describing. Later, I brought the activity visuals to an IEP meeting. The visuals showed Billy Ray actively involved in feeding his horse. I could see the surprise on the faces of several team members. Some of them commented on how he looked substantially independent while performing those tasks. Others admitted they would not have believed he could do that level of activity had they not seen the pictures. Two professionals made appointments to come to our home to observe some of the other things he could do. Unfortunately, sometimes we have to prove our children to others.[16]

The reason for the difference in behavior was that Billy Ray was not able to handle sedentary activities. He needed active tasks to help him control his behavior. The Billy Ray the teacher and others saw was clouded by the inappropriateness of the environment and activities.

Unfortunately, parents often have to fight the red tape and policies to advocate for their children's rights. If possible, when working with your child to plan for his future, try to be realistic but not get stuck on the fight that may lie ahead. As you think of potential goals, to the highest degree possible try to think about what he wants. Modifications may be required to make the goals obtainable, but start by doing your best to ascertain what would make him happiest.

In a recent phone conversation with Sue Rubin's mother, Rita, she credited their school district for Sue's successful transition. However, it appears to me that Rita was very skilled at team-building advocacy as well.

This can be a fight. But if you handle it as though it is physical combat, the chances of getting appropriate services will be reduced. You may be able to rationalize your anger, but it won't solve anything in the end. Goals will be set and achieved only through team-building advocacy and helping the team to see your adult child for who he is.

Appendix C of this book contains an article entitled "Team-Building Advocacy" from my website, www.parentingyourcomplexchild.com. You may find it helpful in planning your approach with the ISP team.

Think about your adult child's goals and remember that even though you have a right to be angry or defensive, once you get angry, the chances of achieving the goals are reduced. I laughingly say that I have learned to advocate with half a tongue because I have had to bite the other half so often! That doesn't mean you have to give up. It just means that if you can find a way to demonstrate your adult child's strengths and abilities without losing your cool, you will be able to accomplish more.

A civil rights movement for people who experience disabilities may not be won in the way equal rights for others would be achieved. As society is able to see an individual for who he is, the right to life, liberty, and the pursuit of happiness may be easier to achieve.

CHAPTER 5

DISCOVERING YOUR
CHILD'S DREAM

YOU HAVE TO START SOMEWHERE

It has been a bit of a struggle to determine which to discuss first—her dream and natural abilities or whether she could receive needed services to accomplish her dream. Policies and programs are changing—sometimes too gradually and sometimes very quickly. However, advocating for a dream means you need to have a dream. Let's start there.

There will be time to wade through what I like to call the "brain fog" (governmental policies and regulations) after determining the dream. There may be lots of options that won't be apparent until after you discover her dream. For purposes of this chapter, we are looking more at goals than actual feasibility. Feasibility is an important consideration in transition planning; however, there are many things that will change during the planning process. Policies regarding funding may change or program availability may change.

A positive change that could occur in the planning is that skills may be attained by your child that you couldn't have anticipated. As she gains skills, her confidence increases, and she may be able to achieve far beyond the goals. Another surprise may be the change in her behavior. If you have caught her interest and begun working with her on activities she enjoys, presenting them in an environment that is more comfortable for her, her entire behavior pattern may change radically for the positive. On the other hand, goals may need to be modified because they end up being a little too much for her. Obviously, you won't want to set goals so high that she will be frustrated. But that doesn't mean not trying anything.

It might seem obvious that an adult who experiences disabilities may need some type of vocational or living situation. Sometimes things that are not so obvious can make all the difference in a person's ability to adapt. Just changing a few conditions may add great meaning to her life. With the right adaptations she may need much less structure than anticipated.

While editing this chapter, I glanced out my window to see the sundial in our front yard. Today it is nearly covered with snow. Only the face itself is peeking through. Talents and potential skills can be like that sundial—all but covered up, their true strengths hidden. By digging out the sundial and placing it in a sunny spot, it is able to function. Maybe your child just needs to be placed in the right situation to bloom and demonstrate what natural skills she possesses.

I like to think about vocational goals first because sometimes residential planning can be adapted to link with them. Additionally, income (or lack thereof) will impact residential planning.

HAPPINESS IS NOT THE SAME FOR EVERYONE

What is involved in your child's pursuit of happiness? First, you'll need to find out what works for her and what is important to her. Happiness for one person may not be the same for another person. A highly social person may enjoy being a hostess in a restaurant or a receptionist in an office, while others prefer to work away from people. Some would like working with animals while others are afraid of them. Some would like the atmosphere in an office while others want to be outside or moving around a lot.

In terms of a residential environment, some people may not want to have their own living situation even though they are perfectly capable of maintaining their own home with minor assistance. Some would find a group home or larger care center with the increased activity and noise far too stimulating or irritating. They may enjoy having one or two roommates but are uncomfortable with more people. Others may need to have their own residence with assistants who are geared only to their personal care and not shared by others.

This chapter is intended to be the beginning of looking for that pursuit of happiness for your child as an individual. She has natural skills, interests, hopes, and dreams. They may be difficult to discover, but she has them. Discovering them may not be the easiest thing you will ever do for your child, but it may be the most rewarding.

CREATING THE TRANSITION PLANNING FILE

It will be helpful to maintain your notes in a file for review as you go along. Get a simple binder with dividers, or any other type of file that works for you. You could make the notes on your computer, printing occasionally and putting them in the binder, or you could just use legal pads or even notebook paper. This file is for you and your child, not for anyone else. Make it as easy on yourself as possible.

This file will include the following:

- Notes from conversations with your child or observations relative to what kind of adult life seems realistic and desirable to her.
- Notes regarding research you do on options and funding sources.
  - Include brochures or information received regarding various programs you have explored.
  - Include one of those plastic filler pages with slots for business cards or a blank sheet of paper to which you will staple cards.
- Draft transition plan.
- Short- and long-term goals.

Make dividers as follows:

- Vocational
- Residential
- Funding/Governmental Benefits
- Draft Transitional Plan
- Short-Term Goals
- Notes

Once you have a file to put your notes in, you are ready to start gleaning information. If you are using the documentation system from Chapter 12 of *Parenting Your Complex Child*, especially the journal, or some other form of journal you keep for your child, a good way to start planning for transitioning is to review as much of that documentation as you can. Gather evaluations, IEPs, notes from teachers or other professionals, and the school/home journal if you maintain one. Grab a notepad and pen, and take notes as you look through available data.

Look for times that she was the happiest and any special skills. If they were associated with any specific activity, make a note about it.

If you are using the transition plan recommended in Chapter 10 of *Parenting Your Complex Child*, you can add a copy of it to this file. You will want to review it to measure her progress in achieving the goals set and to determine whether the goals still seem appropriate to your child as an adult. It may well need at least some minor revisions as you go along.

VOCATIONAL CONSIDERATIONS—FINDING THE NATURAL SKILLS

When I think of finding something that fits well for my own son, I wish for him to be as happy in his job as a man we used to see in the building where Billy Ray's psychiatrist had his office. I don't know his name (we will call him Steve) but the memory of Steve's joy is permanently etched in my memory.

Steve drove an electric wheelchair with an insulated box built on the back. The box had slots to hold coffee cups and other containers. And it displayed a sign with the name of a neighborhood espresso and deli restaurant. Steve delivered coffee and deli items to neighboring office buildings. Sometimes his raincoat literally dripped heavy Oregon rain, but his joyous noise was never diminished. I never heard him to talk to anyone with words, but he communicated his joy with his laughter and other happy sounds. I asked him one day if he liked his job. He literally roared with laughter and his face beamed. He reacted similarly when greeting his customers.

Adapting conditions and working with customers must have taken much work on the part of a skills trainer, business owner, and/or parents. The only functional movement I observed Steve use was one hand with which drove his wheelchair and used a baton to operate the elevator and front door. He didn't make change or hand customers their orders. I don't know if customers had accounts or if there was a place for them to deposit their money. He must have had skills that were not obvious. For example, his vision and sense of direction must have been good, because the coffee shop was in the strip mall in the next block from the office building where we regularly saw him. He had to cross a busy intersection and make his way through several parking lots; his memory had to be good because of all the various offices he delivered to (we never saw a sheet with written instructions or directions). There were certainly many details to be worked out in order for the system to work for Steve. It also likely took lots of investigation to determine that this job was something Steve would enjoy. The result of that adapting was not only Steve's joy but the obvious joy he brought to his customers and others he met in the buildings. Most of us know people who experience much less joy in their vocation than Steve demonstrated in his.

As stated, sorting was always a goal put on Billy Ray's IEP. It was as though there was a predetermined plan for him someday to get a job in a sheltered workshop assembly line. Neither he nor I were consulted about this. It was simply expected. At that time, kids who experienced at least moderate disabilities grew up to work in sheltered workshops. That was the expected goal.

During his sophomore year in high school, Billy Ray was having difficulty in his classroom. It was decided that he might do better in a joint placement with a training center nearby instead of remaining in the classroom all day. The training center placement primarily consisted of an assembly line.

For the most part, this was assembly of hospital admittance packs (bath accessories, water bottles, facial tissues, etc.). Several tables were placed together in a U shape. A bath pan would be passed around the line and each person would put an item in it. During my visits, I observed long periods of time between when pans came around to Billy Ray. He was supposed to remain seated while waiting. He was not comfortable sitting still for even short periods of time, let alone for long periods in between tasks. His behavior demonstrated that the placement was not working for him.

Some people in that assembly line seemed to genuinely enjoy the process. They looked happy. Billy Ray and others appeared miserable. While those types of programs work for some people, others are forced into them because it is easier to develop programs that serve a large group of people than to create individualized vocational experiences that each person loves and in which he or she will thrive.

Too often, older kids and adults are placed into vocational programs because of what is available, not because of what works for the individual. When it doesn't work out for one reason or another, they are homebound or forced into other vocational placements that may be equally frustrating to them.

During a phone conversation with noted speaker and writer Temple Grandin, PhD (one of the world's most accomplished adults who experience autism, Dr. Grandin is well known for her work on the design of livestock handling facilities), I mentioned that it seemed most programs were for higher-functioning people, and those who might be considered lower functioning were pushed into systems that were frustrating. Dr. Grandin told me that at the various conferences where she spoke, she was meeting more and more higher-functioning people capable of working, but who were staying home drawing SSI benefits because they were unable to find what worked for them. Dr. Grandin and Kate Duffy co-authored *Developing Talents*[17] to help with that situation.

Finding meaningful work for people who function on the lower end of the scale appears more difficult than for those at the higher end. However, I believe part of it may be the lack of an opportunity for students to demonstrate their skills, and part of it may be the masking of skills because of inappropriate programs or environments. I strongly believe that many people have hidden skills that will show themselves if the effort is made to reveal them.

Success and performance are strongly impacted by the comfort level in the work environment. If behavior in one setting is undesirable, it is difficult to convince vocational counselors or program personnel that your child may do well in another setting. Documentation, visuals, and creating positive opportunities to demonstrate skills or abilities will help advocate for that.

There are tests that can be administered to show abilities for certain professions. If they are available to your child and she cooperates well, that may be very helpful at some point. However, if your child is not able to verbalize interest, your observations are important to the tester as well.

I love that Dr. Beth Mount, in her book *Person-Centered Planning: Finding Directions for Change Using Personal Futures Planning,* says that a system-centered plan "invests in standardized testing and assessments. Depends on professionals to make judgments." While person-centered plans "Spend(s) time getting to know people. Depend(s) on people, families, and direct service workers to build good descriptions."[18] There is so much more that can be known about a person than will come out in testing. Input from the person, her parents, friends, and family is vital. That doesn't mean there is anything wrong with doing testing, but I don't see it as the absolute final word on planning for your adult child.

Depending on the stage of your child or adult child's life when you are reading this, there is much you can do to help the process long before vocational testing is available. There are questions you can consider about what she seems happiest doing and conversations that you may be able to have with her. Some things you will just notice over time.

In *Developing Talents*, Dr. Grandin and Ms. Duffy write:

Parents play the most important role in the task of getting youths on the autism spectrum ready for the job world. If you are the parent of a child on the autism spectrum, help your child cultivate his or her strengths early on. How? By observing and listening and an awful lot of reflection. Notice his or her interests and passions—even if they seem a little off the wall or different. If your youngster is a whiz at taking things apart, be sure to have plenty of Legos at home. Save boxes so your daughter can build a city, a grocery store or sculpture. For older children, science project kits are recommended. If you find your son plopped down on the ground studying an ant trail, get down with him and watch those ants at work. Learn about the natural world with him, check out books from the library, spend time outdoors walking that ant trail. Be delighted if your child is attracted to something like ants. With an interest in nature, children become explorers opening up their lives even more.[19]

I often wonder about Steve, the man who delivered coffee from his electric wheelchair. How did they determine he would get so much joy in this job? Did his parents own the coffee shop and make a place for him? Did he have an extraordinarily creative skills trainer? I tried to find him again to ask the coffee shop owner those questions, but they have moved or closed now. I imagine that it was lots of trial and error and training.

When I married Larry, he lived on a small farm and had two horses. Billy Ray loved feeding the horses and even shoveling out the barn. A family friend, who also happened to be a 4-H leader, commented that when Billy Ray grew up there would be no problem finding a job cleaning the barn and feeding the horses because many farmers were unable to find people willing to do that type of work. Some of those types of jobs even have living arrangements such as small cabins, mobile homes, or bunkhouses on the property for staff to occupy. If the individual is able to handle at least semi-independence, this might work very well. Billy Ray's health problems have gotten in the way of that possibility now; otherwise, it might have been something he would have enjoyed as an adult job.

As quoted earlier, you can help by observing, listening, and doing lots of reflecting. Let's start now, regardless of whether your child is 10 or 35 years old. Use journals and/or think about activities she has done over the years. Try answering some of the following questions and making notes as you go:

- What activity does she seem happiest doing? You might list that she is happiest cooking with Mom or Dad. Maybe she is happiest playing with her animals? Maybe she loves dismantling things? Is there one task she loves doing at school or home that she seems to enjoy most? Note any possibilities that come to mind while thinking about this.

- Are there some obvious natural abilities to certain tasks that she demonstrates?

- Has she done special assignments or projects in school that could be adapted to some kind of vocational experience?

- What is her physical strength and interest in tasks that involve heavy lifting? This can be anything from hoisting her bicycle onto a bike rack to lifting she has done in projects around the house or school. If she enjoys it and is capable of doing it, take note.

- Is there an activity that she is more independent doing than other things? If so, can you relate that activity to a potential job?

Making a list of skills she has may give you some insight too. As she goes through her routine each day, make a list of everything she is able to do. Include even the simplest things that she does so automatically you may not really notice until you make an effort to be more observant for a few days. You can even create a simple chart to consider what jobs would use those skills. If she has several skills that would apply to a certain job and she seems to enjoy performing those tasks, it may give you some idea of the appropriateness of the job for her.

Here are just a few examples of skill and job matching:

- Enjoys a computer and able to do several tasks independently:
  - With the right training she may enjoy some kind of computer work done at a job site or from home. For example, my aunt and her husband both require a great deal of assistance in their daily lives, but they can use the computer. Neither one is able to type long documents fast enough to be a transcriber, but they can make address labels for customers, and they had their own small business doing just that.
- Likes to answer the phone:
  - With the right kind of training she may be a receptionist or telephone operator if she is able to speak clearly enough.
- Very social and loves to be with people:
  - Perhaps she would enjoy being a restaurant hostess.
  - Or a tour guide in a museum, gallery, or zoo.
- Loves animals and very responsible at taking care of them:
  - She may enjoy working on a farm, in a kennel, pet store, or veterinary office.
  - Depending on her educational skills, perhaps she could go to school to be a veterinary assistant.

- Perhaps (even with the help of support staff if she can't do it independently) she could clean cages, stack pet food, or stock supplies on store shelves.
- Enjoys housework:
  - She might like working on a janitorial crew, being a motel maid, or doing housework for individuals.
- Likes to do laundry:
  - She might like to work in a professional laundry, dry cleaners, or laundromat.

After contemplation, prepare to talk to your child or adult child about his or her wishes or dreams. Even if she is not substantially verbal, you can have a conversation about what it means to have a job and what kinds of things she might like to do. Pictures of people doing various jobs may help her focus on your discussion. Don't just include jobs that you think she would like. She may very well surprise you by bringing up something you never even considered. If so, discuss with her what is involved in the job and consider if she can be trained for the skills necessary, either in school, at home, or in some other training program.

With a picture of someone performing each job, list as many of the tasks involved in that job as you can think of. Don't be afraid to include things that you know she doesn't like to do. She needs to have a realistic picture in her mind of what each job would entail.

Do not push it too far the first time, if she seems disinterested in the conversation or tires easily. Put things away and bring them out a few days later when her interest may be greater.

If there is hesitance to discuss transitioning into work or a residential setting, observe whether it might be fear of leaving you. Provide necessary reassurance that you will be a part of helping her if she needs you to advocate or be there for her.

IT MUST BE REALISTIC

Be realistic in your considerations. There must be a balance. You don't want to encourage your child beyond what is realistic or discourage her from trying due to fear of failure. Always consider adaptive methods or equipment that may turn something she can't do into something she can.

When Billy Ray was in fifth grade, I was room mother. As I was arriving with goodies for a class party, the students were gathered in a circle. They had been given lists of careers to choose from. They were going around the circle to share what career they wanted as adults. One boy, who seemed unable to focus on anything for long, stated he wanted to be a geologist when he grew up. A girl who appeared to have significant learning delays as well as a physical disability stated she wanted to be a nurse. Others chose careers that seemed unrealistic. When they got around to Billy Ray, he said he wanted to be a dishwasher in Robbie's Restaurant (a little restaurant in our neighborhood at that time). I remember thinking that while this was not even on the list, it was probably the most achievable goal of any expressed by the students.

Interestingly enough, when I reviewed the list of careers later, the vast majority of them would have required higher education. This class was a life skills class. Many of the students were probably considered "trainable" as opposed to "educatable." I don't know how many of them were able to read. Billy Ray was not being provided academics such as reading and math that would have allowed him to attain a higher education. (You can read the frustration of that story in *Parenting Your Complex Child*.)

There are factors to consider besides skills. One important consideration is the ability to handle the environment required by the job. Some would not be able to handle a noisy environment. Others would find too many fluorescent lights triggering difficult behaviors or confusion.

Dr. Grandin points out that many people on the autism spectrum are very good at technical jobs but not so good at social interactions. For the most part, social interactions in the workplace are something that can be worked on with a job coach, parents, or other support. Some skills would not be trainable for every person.

The degree of supervision needed will be an important consideration as well. Some programs have job coaches and supervisors to assist participants. Other jobs require total independence. You will have to look at what type of job and how much assistance will be needed. Then you will have to ascertain if the level of assistance would be available in that type of job.

Recently, we had two important pieces of furniture bite the dust in our house, and we had deliveries from the furniture store. In both cases, the driver of the delivery truck had assistants who were in training. The driver was showing the assistant how to pick up furniture. In the case of Billy Ray's new mattress, the driver was showing the assistant how to pick it up through the plastic cover and use the plastic to protect the mattress so it wouldn't get dirty handprints on it. Watching this, it occurred to me that there are probably many delivery jobs that people with special needs would be strong enough to do and enjoy. It is something that Billy Ray would likely enjoy.

Just being observant in day-to-day life, you may well see things you realize might be something your adult child is capable of and may enjoy. With the right advocating and negotiating, a plan may be worked out that will be good for both your child and an employer.

Additionally, the ability to take care of personal needs while in the work environment is a consideration. If she can perform the work, but not care for her own personal needs (toileting, remembering to take medication if necessary, getting lunch, etc.), she would need an assistant at least periodically throughout the day. That may work in certain job sites, but not in others. And funding for a part-time assistant may or may not be available, depending on the circumstances.

As stated, Billy Ray loves being with horses, feeding them and cleaning up after them. He could control his behavior at that point—at least long enough to work with his horses. This seemed a real potential for him when he was about 13. Since that time he has developed increasing physical issues. He is not always able to communicate verbally when he is in pain. He often communicates his discomfort by his behavior, which can be aggressive. On occasion he has communicated that by striking his horse. This could be dangerous. Additionally, he no longer has the energy necessary for that kind of work. As much as he would enjoy the work, it is not realistic for him any more. While working with horses may not be realistic now, there are many ways to adapt his love of animals to a job he would enjoy and is able to do.

Careers that require a college education are more and more workable for persons with disabilities. Vocational schools may be a good option as well. Fortunately, more children with disabilities are being taught to read than when Billy Ray was in school. There are programs that will provide an aide to go with a student to school and assist in whatever way is necessary.

RESIDENTIAL DREAM

This must be realistic too. Certainly you want her to have a home life that will make her happy but there are multiple things to consider:

- Can she live independently with some help?
    - Would she be comfortable alone for long periods of time?
    - If she needs to take medication, would she be able to self-medicate safely?
    - Could she call 911 and actually get out of the house in the event of a fire or know how to deal with another emergency?
    - Can she take care of her own personal care and maintain reasonable housekeeping chores?
- Is there funding available for full-time help if that is what she needs to live in her own home?
- Does she require special medical treatment?
    - Can it be provided by someone coming into her home?
- Will she require a more structured residential program such as a group home, residential care center, or adult foster home?
    - Will she be able to tolerate being in a larger environment, or will she need to have a specially developed foster home?

There may be ways to creatively include both vocational and residential planning. Sometimes living arrangements can be made to coincide with vocational arrangements. As previously mentioned, sometimes jobs have trailers or cabins for the employees. They may even provide meals. If she is able to basically take care of herself and handle her own medications, she may be able to live at the site where she works.

In an assisted living facility where I used to visit a client, there was a man who answered the phone and served as receptionist for several hours a day. He used a wheelchair and needed assistance with his own care. However, he was very social and had a very nice speaking voice. He told me that he had arranged a deal where he could work to offset the cost of some of his care. It made him proud that he was able to work and not depend entirely on the government or family members.

For purposes of this chapter, be extra observant of your adult child's skills, review as much of the data you have collected, and try to come up with some ideas for discussion with your son or daughter. After discussion(s) with your son or daughter, try to note and save his or her wishes for creating a transition plan after you have researched the options. These notes will become the early draft of your child's dream. The dream will undoubtedly be revised as you research the options in the next chapter, but you will have made a good start with your child.

RESEARCHING
THE OPTIONS

MORE THAN YOU EVER WANTED TO LEARN ABOUT
POLICIES, PROGRAMS, AND RED TAPE

Support for an adult with special needs can be very complicated. Maybe by working, he can earn enough money to pay for an apartment, but not enough to pay for medications and medical care. If he gets supplemental income from Social Security and wants to marry, he could lose part of the benefits that are important to his survival. If he gets disability income as a disabled adult child (DAC), he may lose all of his benefits if he marries—unless he marries another DAC. Checking out such issues is vital before taking action to create a living/work situation for an adult with disabilities.

In the United States, funding and support for programs tend to change from good to bad and back again. Policies that make a plan feasible may change at any given time; you can be in violation without even knowing it! Lawmakers seem to be trying to improve the lives of persons who experience disabilities. The American with Disabilities Act of 1990 was supposed to make accommodations. But it hasn't always worked out that way. And that has led to some controversy.

In determining whether your son or daughter's dream is feasible, you will likely have to learn more about "the system" than you ever dreamed existed. Even if he is high functioning enough to learn to be a self-advocate, he is going to need a lot of help researching programs, funding sources, policies, and red tape. You will have to learn the policies and procedures to help him learn them.

My son's service budget for in-home support (federal, state, and county monies), which I don't consider to be extensive given his complexities and all the services that are provided by his family which could be requested if he were not at home, was initially established while we lived in another county of this state. The budget accompanied him to the new county. I have heard more than once since moving here that Billy Ray's budget is substantially higher than most in this area. But rather than Billy Ray's budget being too high, I believe that other families may not understand their adult child's eligibility and/or didn't advocate for services to which they may be entitled.

As stated, Dr. Temple Grandin shared her frustration at seeing person after person who, although able to work, sat home collecting SSI. With assistance in developing skills to find an appropriate job, many people who experience disabilities could become self-supporting and need little, if any, government assistance. I have thought about that a great deal since my conversation with Dr. Grandin. I believe this is true for people who function at many different levels—not just the high functioning.

It would be impossible for this book to cover every option or regulation in every area of the United States. We cannot walk you through every waiver or appeal. But hopefully we can provide some ideas at how to cut through the red tape and get funding for your adult child's vocational, residential, and other services.

Potential funding sources may include the following.

PRIVATE FUNDING

Part or all of the support may be provided by private sources such as:

- A special needs trust by parents, grandparents, or other family members (see Chapter 9, "Estate Planning," for more discussion on coordinating special needs trusts with governmental benefits).

- Earnings from employment if your son or daughter earns enough to provide for support.

GOVERNMENT FUNDING

This can be from one governmental source or several. Here are a few examples:

- Supplemental Security Income (SSI): This is a small monthly benefit from the Social Security Administration based on disability. While not generally enough to live on without other funding sources, eligibility for SSI is often important to get other benefits.

- Medical plan: This can be a state health plan (low-income health coverage that is usually funded by both state and federal resources); it can also be Medicare from Social Security or in combination with state plans.

- Food stamps: These are based on income but take high medical expenses, etc., into consideration.

- Reduced rent programs: These are usually administered through the local housing authority; generally, rent is based on income and disability.

- In-home supports: This can come in a variety of services such as:
  - Independent living trainer: Someone who will come weekly or biweekly to check on a person, assist with specified needs, or provide specific training as identified in the Individual Service Plan.
  - Short-term assistant: Someone who will come to assist with bathing or other needs for care and/or recreation.
  - Full-time support staff: Around-the-clock and/or live-in staff to provide care and protection if it is determined that a person might otherwise be unsafe or unable to provide self-care.

- Vocational rehabilitation services: These services could include
  - Assistance in finding a vocational placement and adapting a work site to the person's needs.
  - Training for employment.

- ○ Providing a job coach to be with the person during work hours or to check in at the work site regularly to assure that things are going well (the degree of frequency will be based on a person's needs for assistance while working).
- Residential support: This could be a group home or another care facility for those who cannot function in their own homes with assistance.

Often there is a combination of funding. For example, in the documentary *Autism Is a World*, by Sue Rubin, Sue's mother shares that Sue receives SSI plus is a Section 8 renter through the Housing Authority (which means she gets rental assistance). She also gets full-time in-home support staff because Sue, who experiences autism, would not be able to get out of her apartment or call 911 in the event of a fire or another emergency. She doesn't say whether Sue gets food stamps, but it would appear likely that she would qualify.

WHERE YOU LIVE MATTERS

Depending on the age of your child when you are doing this planning, and the area where you live, researching the options may be done somewhat differently. For example, if you are planning for a 14-year-old, you may not be able to establish his eligibility for certain programs until he is 18. However, it may be possible to put him on a waiting list even though he is not ready for the program you are exploring. On the other hand, if your child is an adult or nearly an adult, you will want to consider options and get him on every appropriate waiting list for services or benefits.

Some of the funds for these services are actually federal monies. However, the states are given the funds to administer according to state policies, as long as they are approved by the federal government. As you can imagine, this often leads to confusing information and incorrect or inconsistent answers to questions. It can be a frustrating experience—and a different experience depending on the state where you reside.

According to the Social Security Act:

Appropriation
Sec.1901. [42 U.S.C. 1396] For the purpose of enabling each State, as far as practicable under the conditions in such State, to furnish (1) medical

assistance on behalf of families with dependent children and of aged, blind, or disabled individuals, whose income and resources are insufficient to meet the costs of necessary medical services, and (2) rehabilitation and other services to help such families and individuals attain or retain capability for independence or self-care, there is hereby authorized to be appropriated for each fiscal year a sum sufficient to carry out the purposes of this title. The sums made available under this section shall be used for making payments to States which have submitted, and had approved by the Secretary, State plans for medical assistance. (From the Social Security Act website, www.ssa.gov/OP_Home/ssact/title19/1901.htm)

It can be very confusing, especially if you move from state to state or sometimes even from county to county.

We just experienced some of that confusion for Billy Ray. Billy Ray receives SSDI because his dad was receiving SSDI at the time of his death (when Billy Ray was 11 years old). Until Billy Ray was 18 he received benefits as a survivor, then he was declared a disabled adult child and continues to collect benefits on his father's claim, except now it is based on his own disability.

Because of his complex medical needs, developmental disabilities, and behavioral concerns, he receives comprehensive in-home services primarily consisting of funding for in-home support staff and a state medical card. We were notified that he must become SSI eligible (whether he receives it or not) to continue to get these services. He is not SSI eligible because his benefit on his father's claim is more than SSI benefits would be. The state's answer to that is that he must pay an "offset"—in other words, the difference between what he would get for SSI and what he receives from his father's claim.

I was talking to a friend who works in developmental services in another county. She said that as a disabled adult child Billy Ray should be exempt from having to pay that offset. I followed up with the state office to figure out which was accurate—what I was told by our county office or what my friend said.

Apparently, the term "disabled adult child" can mean different things in different agencies. Billy Ray is a DAC for Social Security purposes. However, he must be classified as a DAC for Medicaid purposes as well. There is a test of five different points to be eligible for that classification. One of the points is that he must have been eligible for SSI at age 18. He was not because he was receiving benefits under his dad's claim before his eighteenth birthday, and it was too much to make him eligible for SSI.

It was explained to me that based on the plan the state created for its Medicaid services, as per the quoted language about appropriation, Billy Ray will not qualify for Medicaid services unless he has a waiver. In order to get the waiver, he must be SSI eligible. So he will have to give the state more than 40 percent of the benefit he received from his father's claim for SSDI.

It can be enough to make your head spin, but it is absolutely necessary to follow up on details with your local agency because, as David C. Stapleton told me in a recent phone interview, "There are several federal agencies involved in providing support to people with disabilities. Federal agencies don't work well together and each agency reports to a different committee."

The services themselves may be the same in one state, but sometimes counties provide those services in a different way. For example, when we lived in one county in Oregon, Billy Ray had a case manager. He really didn't need much help from the case manager because things were going smoothly, and I handled most details myself. After we moved to another county, he developed behavior issues created by medical concerns and structure problems in a new classroom. I believed that school regulations were being violated and requested case management assistance. I was told that the county we then lived in didn't open cases on kids in school because the school basically acted as case manager.

ESTABLISHING CONTACT WITH YOUR LOCAL AGENCY

Thus, I am providing *general* information about federal programs and ideas to help you formulate goals and questions. You will then be prepared to go into the agency that represents adults with disabilities in your area. If your child doesn't have a case manager, ask for an intake appointment. Tell the receptionist that you just want to come in and ascertain options so that you can begin planning. The agency may or may not open a case at that point.

At the appointment be prepared with the following information about your child or adult child:

- What kind of assistance or services you expect to be required. For example,

- Semi-independent living program (someone to assist in his own home with things like grocery shopping, help in managing his financial matters, training in certain aspects of housekeeping, transportation, etc., as well as checking on him periodically to assure all is going well).
- Vocational training or placement.
  - Residential placement, if necessary.
  - Medical card.
  - In-home support staff and how many hours in a week.

Find out whether you need to check in with other agencies or if services can be coordinated through the agency's providing case management staff. Also ask about waiting lists.

While the agency may be more than willing to talk about program services, there may be some hesitance to give you specific programs that provide vocational and residential services. Tell the intake worker or case manager that you desire to visit comparable programs to get an idea of how to work with your child or adult child to prepare him for transitioning. Assure the case manager that you won't try to make arrangements or get on an agency waiting list if it is not appropriate to do so (sometimes waiting lists for programs supported through county funding must be handled by the agency).

VOCATIONAL PROGRAMS

Armed with the list of programs that your state or county agency has provided you, it may be helpful for you to visit the programs that seem like possible fits based on your child's goal. Depending on the situation, you might visit without him the first time and then bring him along on a subsequent visit. That way you can ascertain how much training it would require and how realistic it is for him. You could then talk to him about how the program will help him reach his goal. When you're assured he has remained interested, take him to visit one or more of the available programs.

It is much easier to evaluate programs and advocate for your child before he is number one on the waiting list for service funding and you must make a selection. The pressure is much more extreme when he's at the top of the list. And by starting early you can get on multiple waiting lists instead of just one. Sometimes, it will be easier to get him into a vocational program than a residential one.

RESIDENTIAL OPTIONS

If you have ascertained that he can live in his own home or with a room-mate, look into the types of living arrangements that are available, such as the following:

- Reduced rent through governmental agencies: Find out what he has to do to qualify. Will his income from the vocational plan be a problem?
- Apartment programs: For example, sometimes there are blocks of apartments with a supervisor living in one apartment. Maybe the supervisor only needs to check to assure he has been taking his meds or keeping himself and his apartment clean. If you had some concern about his ability to function in his own apartment, this might be a good starting point.

- Family-owned property: Is there a property that could be transferred into a trust and then leased to him at a reduced rent without affecting his eligibility for governmental programs?
- Combining residence with work: For example, what if he couldn't live alone but wanted to do janitorial or kitchen work, or even minor office work in an assisted living facility or a nursing home? Could he exchange part or all of that for an assisted living apartment where he could also get some care and supervision such as medication management?
- Semi-independent living programs: A situation where someone will come by his apartment regularly for an agreed-upon amount of time to ensure safety and security as well as take him grocery shopping or to medical appointments if necessary.

In general, I would advise thinking about vocational programs first because it is often easier to adapt living arrangements to coincide with work than vice versa.

OTHER THINGS TO CONSIDER

In helping your child plan for a happy adult life, there are things you will need to consider besides just where he will live and work.

- Can he tolerate a group setting even if he is not able to be independent? Some would need absolute structure and reasonable quiet that wouldn't be possible in a group setting.
- Would he be able to communicate discomfort with the residential environment (this would include place, people, schedule, and even arrangement of equipment or furnishings) and with the vocational experience? Many adults who are able to speak still have difficulty in communicating their needs.
- Security issues: Is he vulnerable to harm? Can you help him to understand the dangers of certain behaviors or does he need more intense protection?
- Does he need any type of adaptive equipment?
  - Does it need to be purchased? How will it be funded? Will it determine the type of environment that he will be able to work or live in? For example, an office building or residence with steps but no elevator may not work for someone using a wheelchair or walker.
  - Simple household tools may need to be adapted and gathered for him if he is going to have an apartment. Billy Ray, for example, loves peeling potatoes, but needs a special potato peeler.

There are so many variances that affect transition into adulthood, including

- The level of assistance your adult child needs.
- Skills of living as well as vocational skills.
- Available and appropriate programs.
- Funding.

Coordinating funding and services can be very complicated. For example, you will have to be very concerned about work programs affecting Social Security benefits because so often other benefits (health plans, housing, and food stamps, for example) are tied in with eligibility for disability benefits through Social Security. In Appendix E, I have included information on some work programs through the U.S. government. With some of those programs a disabled adult can receive free hospital insurance through Medicare for 93 months after going to work. After the initial 93 months, he may be eligible to buy hospital insurance through Medicare (the rate was $407 per month for 2007) and medical insurance (the rate was $93.50 per month for 2007).

Thus, in addition to looking at what kind of vocational or residential dream will make him happy, there are multiple other things to consider. They include medical insurance and the ability to pay for other needs that might not be covered if he earns too much working.

Having listened to your adult child's wishes, reviewed the options with your local programs, and given a lot of thought to whether they all fit together for a safe and happy life, you are ready to start creating a plan and the goals to achieve it.

There are many things to consider. At first it will probably seem overwhelming. Think of it as creating a beautiful puzzle. One piece doesn't seem to fit, so you keep trying, and pretty soon you find the placement that fits just right.

For example, sometimes when appropriate vocational programs don't work or would affect eligibility for disability benefits, you may find a volunteer program that fits nicely. In Billy Ray's case, he is not able to participate in regular employment for a number of reasons. But he can do short activities and very much enjoys serving others and working. He is able to deliver Meals on Wheels to elderly or disabled people who are housebound. His stepfather or support staff person accompanies him for this activity. He thoroughly enjoys seeing the people on his route and they enjoy him very much, too. It does not affect his benefits and it works for him.

When researching the options, one thing that you will need to ask is what happens if the plan is not in place by the time you or your spouse is no longer able to provide care. There may be reasons why the actual transition has to be delayed. Funding is likely the biggest reason. If the plan is to have 24-hour in-home staff, it might not be granted as long as the parents are participating. Sometimes the health of the adult child is a factor. It may be necessary to have a backup plan such as the one in Appendix A for unplanned emergencies.

The plan will vary greatly by what you determine his independence is and what his needs will be. If you don't feel that he is able to adapt to the options your local agency suggests and is not able to be independent enough to live alone, you will have to be creative in planning. Don't get stuck accepting the agency suggestions as your only options. Consider what your adult child needs and create a plan based on his needs. Advocate for as close to that plan as possible. It may require some compromise.

CHAPTER 7

DRAFTING A
TRANSITIONAL PLAN

WRITING THE PLAN

We began thinking about transition planning early in Billy Ray's life. That was because we had to make some financial decisions. It was felt that he could strongly benefit from intense (and expensive) speech therapy that was not available through our HMO. We could not afford the monthly cost of the therapy and of the premiums to fund an insurance trust to provide care after we were gone. We had to look at the degree of independence that was reasonable to expect him to achieve.

Billy Ray had bloomed. He learned so fast after coming to us at 15 months old, the developmental pediatrician felt it likely that he could become semi-independent as an adult. Thus, we elected to get the therapy. At 14 years old he experienced an unexpected deterioration in his ability to function (see *Parenting Your Complex Child* for the whole story of that change). It was necessary to rethink his transition plan entirely.

Presently, he remains in our home because of multiple medical problems. Transition has been slowed or stopped numerous times because of his changing health and care needs. However, there are many things that can be done to prepare him for transition while he is still in the nest. We are basically starting again, just as many of you are.

In Billy Ray's case it is highly unlikely that he would adjust to a residential situation with many fellow residents. He is easily stimulated by behavior or noise from others. Additionally, his behaviors and noise can set others off. He likes people and would likely enjoy sharing a home with one or two roommates, as long as it was arranged so that he could have enough of his own space and time with his own assistant, and as long as the personalities of his roommate(s) and their staff match his personality.

Your child may be able to live in her own apartment with someone checking in to assist with grocery shopping, bill-paying, and other activities. Others will need some sort of residential care.

The degree and type of planning will vary greatly by the needs and independence of your adult child. We will look at three very different plans here. Chances are that your adult child's plan will fall somewhere in between. These examples are meant to highlight the concept of adapting to the individual desires and needs of your adult child.

Judy will ultimately be fairly independent while Zach will need substantially more assistance built into his plan. Denny will need less assistance outside of his facility, but will still need the protection of having friends and family remain involved and aware of his circumstances; he needs their friendship too. The protections built into each plan have similarities and differences. Self-confidence and the highest degree of independence possible will be important to all, even though it will be at different levels and will be built into the plans by different methods.

We will create a transitional plan basically consisting of long-term goals. You can create it in any format that works for you. I like to maintain it on the computer so I can change it as circumstances merit. But ease of use is more important than format. In the next chapter, we will begin to create short-term goals based on the long-term goals we'll discuss here.

Perhaps writing a paragraph or two describing what it will feel like when all the goals are accomplished for her may help to make it clear for you and your child. Include details you know will be important to her. It might read something like this:

> Judy would like to have an apartment or a house with another girl when she moves out of Mom and Dad's house. She wants to have her own bed-

room and to have a cat. Judy would like to work in a laundromat. She wants to be able to go bowling, go to church, and go out for pizza.

After you write it out with Judy and read it together, she may have other things to add. Have pictures available for her to use if she is nonverbal. It may be good to wait a few days after writing it, then go over it with her again in case other things have come to mind for her and for you. If it is still in line with your thinking and hers, you can go on to prepare the transitional plan.

Break down the goals into sections such as:

- Residential
- Vocational
- Financial

In thinking about the residential goals, Judy expresses a desire to have a roommate when she moves into her own home. The easiest thing will be if she has had a long-term friend with whom she is very comfortable. However, a comfortable relationship can be established during the transition. Add a transition goal to plan for a roommate. When creating short-term goals, you can list the ways that you will help her to establish a relationship with someone she would be comfortable sharing her home with.

You will need to ascertain the degree of assistance needed by looking at such things as whether she can do her own housekeeping, handle transportation needs, shop, and schedule appointments. Will she need a semi-independent-living trainer to come in and support her with certain tasks in her home? How much help will she need? Create goals for needed assistance.

A transitional plan for Judy might look like this:

TRANSITIONAL PLAN FOR JUDY

Statement of Judy's Goal

Judy would like to have an apartment or a house with another girl when she moves out of Mom and Dad's house. She wants to have her own bedroom and to have a cat. Judy would like to work in a laundromat. She wants to be able to go bowling, go to church, and go out for pizza.

Residential Goals

1. Judy will find an apartment or house through the Housing Authority.
2. Judy will need the following assistance in her home.
    A. Semi-independent-living trainer
        1) Assure Judy has skills necessary to maintain her home. Train in additional tasks or activities that are appropriate for Judy to do.
        2) Assist with menu planning, preparing a grocery list, and grocery shopping.
        3) Assist with budgeting, banking, and bill-paying as needed.
    B. Health assistant
        1) Determine if assistance is needed with self-care and other health needs.
        2) Ensure medical appointments are scheduled and transportation available. Accompany Judy if requested.
        3) Ensure medications are being taken appropriately, refilled, and picked up or delivered as needed.
    C. Advocate assistant (Judy will be a self-advocate)
        1) Discuss with Judy any changes she would like in her plan.
        2) Assist in research of policies if necessary.
        3) Attend meetings with Judy if desired by Judy.
        4) Provide any other assistance such as arranging transportation, having photocopies made, etc., that Judy might need for her meetings or self-advocating.
    D. Case manager–consultant
        1) Ensure needed staffing is available to Judy.
        2) Periodically check in with Judy to ensure things are working as Judy desires.
        3) Assure that Judy is getting access to friends and family and recreation to the degree she desires.
3. A roommate that Judy is compatible with will be located.
4. Judy will learn to maintain her home.

5. Judy will learn to care for her cat.

Vocational Goals

1. Judy will apply to Vocational Rehabilitation for placement and/or a job coach.
2. Judy and her case manager will work with her Voc Rehab worker to ensure that her work earnings do not exceed the amount allowed to continue her SSI eligibility or eligibility for other services that can't be replaced by her earnings.

Financial Goals

1. Judy will apply for SSI.
2. Judy will apply for food stamps and a medical card through Medicaid.
3. Judy will apply for rent reduction through the Housing Authority.

General Goals

1. Judy will be trained to be a self-advocate.
2. Aunt Clarissa will assist Judy with advocating needs (such as research, letting Judy practice, attending meetings if Judy wishes, etc.) as necessary.
3. Susan (Judy's cousin) will maintain her story and assist with advocating when needed.

If your child is still in school when you are doing the transitional plan, you may want to take a closer look at this point relative to the skills that will be necessary for her to achieve the transitional goals. Figure 7.1 is a sample list of skills and abilities that would be necessary for someone to live safely in her own home. Column 3 is a list of IEP goals that could be requested to assist in preparing her for transition. Obviously, some of the training in things such as personal hygiene will be more appropriate at home, but there are many ways that school can help. For example, home economics classes go a long way toward teaching someone to cook for herself.

A transitional plan for my son, Billy Ray, must be more detailed because he is not able to advocate for himself or communicate his concerns or needs. His behavior is impacted by triggers from his environment as well as medical issues that have recently popped up. The following is a transition plan that is

FIGURE 7.1   Skills necessary for independent living with SILP trainer.

Skill/Ability	Subskill Needed	IEP Goals
Able to get help	Telephone skills	Number recognition 911 use Ability to find phone number from list or phone book Basic operating of a telephone and/or answering machine
Ability to medicate self	Able to tell time or understand some type of alarm system for when to take the medications	Time-telling skills
Basic self-care skills	Proper hygiene Basic cooking skills Basic housekeeping skills	 Simple meal preparation, especially breakfast and making a sack lunch Use of a microwave and range This may or may not be offered in school programs—IEP goals would depend on whether there is a life-skills program in your child's school
Basic home safety	Locking doors and windows Knowledge of who is allowed entrance to his home Fire safety	 Stranger-danger program Avoiding fires Training in use of fire extinguisher for small fires Concept of when to get the fire extinguisher and when to get out of the building

Excerpt used by permission of the publisher from *Parenting Your Complex Child* by Peggy Lou Morgan. © 2006 Peggy Lou Morgan, published by AMACOM, division of American Management Association, New York. *www.amacombooks.org*

similar to Billy Ray's. I am using a different name because I want to add other things for illustration as well as to protect Billy Ray's privacy.

TRANSITIONAL PLAN FOR ZACH

Statement of Zach's Goal

Zach will need consistent full-time care. He will be assisted by in-home support staff in his family home or a rented house. His mother will train and supervise his staff to provide consistent care for him. He will require active involvement of a consultant when Mom is no longer available for staff training and to ensure followup of medical care.

Zach will not be able to handle specific vocational programs because of health problems that affect his energy. However, he will do volunteer and recreational activities as tolerated. He will be actively involved with his church, Special Olympics, and his friends/family.

Residential Goals

1. Zach will eventually live in his family home that will be held in a special needs trust. In the beginning he may need to find an apartment or house through the Housing Authority.

2. Zach will need the following assistance in his home.

   A. Case manager–consultant: Will be trained by Mom and/or provided documentation to assist in getting to know Zach and his specific needs for care and comfort.

      1) Ensure needed staffing is available and trained for Zach's care.

      2) Supervise staff to assure consistency in schedule and environment to avoid triggers to behavior issues.

      3) Maintain contact with primary medical care provider to ensure Zach's health and work with in-home support staff or a health aide to assure medical procedures are followed consistently and documentation done for medical provider as requested.

      4) Maintain contact with advocate and county case manager (or other governmental case management personnel).

      5) Coordinate participation in church services/activities, volunteer and recreational activities as tolerated, activities with family and friends, etc.

    6) Ensure visuals and schedules are prepared and available to Zach in the format best for his comfort and security.

  B. Zach will learn to maintain his home with help from his in-home support staff.

  C. Zach will care for his service dog with help from in-home support staff.

Vocational Goals

1. Zach will continue to do Meals on Wheels route as a volunteer.
2. Zach will do other volunteer and recreational activities as tolerated.

Financial Goals

1. Zach will continue to receive benefits from his father's SSDI claim.
2. Zach will continue to receive state health plan and Medicare as his primary health insurance.
3. Zach's guardian will apply for food stamps for him.
4. If necessary, Zach will apply for rent reduction through the Housing Authority.
5. Zach may not need a conservator. There is a trust under his mother's will, and the guardian should be able to manage his limited funds. However, if he should need a conservator to manage his funds, there is a nomination in his mother's will.

General Goals

1. Zach will need a guardian. This will be arranged as provided in his mother's estate plan.
2. Zach's personal advocate will be his friend, Suzanne.
3. His niece Wendy will maintain Zach's story and assist with advocating as needed.
4. Given the difficulty in maintaining staff full time, a backup plan will be established to have friends or family who could either move into Zach's home with him or have Zach move into their home. This plan will be made available to the case manager and Mom's attorney as well as placed in the estate planning file. (See Sample Emergency Backup Plan in Appendix A and Sample Caregiver's Manual in Appendix B.

TRANSITIONAL PLAN FOR DENNY

Statement of Denny's Goals

Denny would like to live in a home similar to Wilderness Cabins, which is a farm with cabins. Each cabin has four residents and a live-in support staff. It is in a country setting but close enough to medical care that Denny's health needs can be easily met. It is close enough to family and friends that Denny will be able to visit and have visitors. There are a full-time nurse and case manager on staff. Denny will be able to have his service dog with him, and there are numerous other pets available, including horses.

Residential Goals

1. Application for services through the County Developmental Disabilities Department has been made with a request for placement at Wilderness Cabins. Denny is on the waiting list for this placement. Anticipated placement is in three to four years.

2. Denny will remain at home with his parents until placement is available at Wilderness Cabins. He will have in-home support staff while his parents are at work.

Vocational Goals

1. While waiting for placement at Wilderness Cabins, Denny and his support staff will participate in volunteer and recreational activities that Denny enjoys.

2. Denny will participate in the local drama club.

3. At Wilderness Cabins, Denny will be trained to care for the farm animals and in other farm chores.

Financial Goals

1. Denny will continue to receive SSI benefits.

2. His guardian will become the representative payee and make payments to Wilderness for his share of the cost.

3. Denny will continue to receive the state health plan and Medicare as his primary health insurance.

4. Denny's supplemental needs will be provided by a special needs trust from his grandparents' trust.

General Goals

1. Denny will need a guardian. This will be arranged as provided in his parents' estate plan.

2. Denny's personal advocate will be his friend, Julie.

3. His sister, Eva, will maintain Denny's story and assist with advocating as needed. Eva will visit at least quarterly and speak to Denny by phone at least weekly. Provisions made in the special needs trust for Denny's benefit will assist Eva with travel expenses to visit Denny and reimburse long-distance calls.

The transition plan for your child forms the long-term goals, giving you a starting point to create short-term goals. It is a good idea to review the plan periodically to see if it is still applicable or if changes are needed.

8

Setting Goals to Accomplish the Transitional Plan

SHORT-TERM GOALS

In Chapter 7, we discussed creating a transitional plan with long-term goals for your adult child. In this chapter, we will use those long-term goals to create short-term goals and implement the transition plan.

Short-term goals, as I see them, consist of building skills and achieving other accomplishments. These can be worked on while you're waiting for the transition to occur. The more prepared your adult child is, the easier it will be for him when he is in his new life. Additionally, he will have more pride in being able to take care of himself and be more independent. Many of these things can be incorporated into his present life if he is still at home with you.

If the transition occurs before all skills are accomplished, they can be worked on with the help of the semi-independent living trainer or a parent. Thus, the plan is a valuable tool even if it is not completely accomplished upon transition.

In your transition planning file, create a page for tasks that you will do and those your adult child will do. As you set short-term goals, there will be some things that you need to do before you are ready to involve him.

As you look at long-term goals in the transition plan, think about the first step toward accomplishing the first goal. For example, Judy wanted to work in a laundromat. A goal for you to accomplish first is to talk with several laundromat managers/owners and maybe the Vocational Rehabilitation counselor about the kinds of tasks Judy will likely need to do.

Let's use Judy's wishes in an example of setting short-term goals.

Vocational

After doing a bit of research with laundromats about the kind of work Judy might be able to do based on her abilities (and without losing benefits), set goals for training she could get while waiting for the plan to be implemented.

Obviously, if she is going to use specialized laundry equipment, this training will have to be provided by a job coach or supervisor since you don't have access to the equipment. However, things like wiping down washers and dryers, emptying lint filters and trash cans, sweeping, and mopping are things that you could work on with her at home.

Set a short-term goal for each task that you will work on with Judy. It is best to work on one task at a time and master that one before adding another. Prioritize the order in which you will work with her on the goals.

Residential

There are things that a person can do in his new home, whether it is a room in a group home or his own apartment. These things may be minor and will probably need to be adapted to the person's abilities. Nevertheless, the sense of doing something to take care of himself is important to his self-esteem.

A personal pet peeve of mine is support staff, trainers, classroom aides, and others who say to a child or adult, Will you help me do this or that—and then basically do the task for the person. If you have read any of my writing, you may have heard this story, but the principle is important and the story bears repeating.

Billy Ray has had two or three in-home support persons who would ask him to help them make his bed. One would arrive at 7 A.M. just about the time he woke up. If he was up, she would tell him to sit in the recliner in his room or send him to the bathroom while she quickly made his bed. That's baloney!!! It's his bed—and making it is his job. We should be helping him do his job, not asking for his help with a job that should be his.

When I help him do this task, I do the first two corners of the fitted sheet (on the top, which are more difficult and frustrate him) and then, hand over hand, we pull the bottom corners in place and straighten out the wrinkles. He doesn't use a top sheet because he gets tangled in it; so we just use a down comforter. He puts the comforter on the bed. I pull one side in place to get it sort of lined up, and then he pulls the other side in place to smooth the wrinkles out. Then he puts the pillows on.

Billy Ray loves to do household chores—with help. I think this is because we have done most things together since he was a small child. Even in the early days, he played with the pots and pans while I was preparing dinner. I don't feel guilty about his working on chores because it's his home too. Plus, it has the added benefit of teaching him to do things in his own home someday. Vacuuming and/or dusting the living room with me is something he enjoys. It would be different if I expected him to fold *my* clothes or clean *my* bedroom. I help him clean the main bathroom (which is primarily his bathroom). But he doesn't do any cleaning in the master bathroom.

Depending on the residential goals you create for your child, teach him to do as much as he can independently. If he uses a wheelchair and can't get it to the head of the bed to do the sheets or bedspread, there may still be parts of the task he can do. Perhaps whoever assists him with his bed could place the pillow on his lap while making the bed, and he can put the pillow back on the bed when it's finished, or maybe he could pull one or two corners of the bedspread into place.

Create goals to teach him as many skills as possible that can be used in whatever type of residential arrangement you expect him to experience as an adult. If, like Judy, he hopes to have his own home with a roommate, think of the tasks he'll need to accomplish to reach that goal. A few examples are the following:

• Maintaining an appropriate schedule so that he is ready for work or other activities

- Personal hygiene
- Self-medicating, if necessary, using bubble packs with the appropriate pills dispensed from the pharmacy
- Menu planning and grocery shopping
- Preparing simple meals
- Housecleaning
- Laundry
- Understanding when to call for help; this would include calling 911, a doctor, a friend or family member, repair personnel, etc.

Some of these tasks may require followup by a semi-independent-living coach when he is in his apartment, but he can learn the basics while in the transitional phase. If he is going to live independently, he is going to need to do as much as possible himself.

It will help to think about one room at a time. For example, think about the kitchen and jot down everything that you can think of that is required to maintain a kitchen. Note tasks that he can already do with a reasonable degree of independence. Create goals to work on the things that you believe he can do, but will require training. Pick one at a time and work with him on it.

You can create those goals in any way that works for you. For example, Figure 8.1 is a partial table about kitchen- and menu-related tasks for Judy. You could list any tasks required in maintaining a kitchen and preparing meals and create a goal for each. If it was something your adult child could already do, you would note that in the comments section, but still include it in activities he would do regularly so that it will eventually be included in his schedule.

When you have finished creating short-term goals for the kitchen, move on to the bathroom and other rooms that will be in his new home.

In teaching skills, think about aspects of the task that might be too difficult for your adult child. He may be able to mop the kitchen floor, but not fill or empty the mop bucket. There are marvelous products available that make such tasks much easier. Most of them are created for speed and ease, but they can be adapted for people with disabilities. There are specially made handles with a flat surface where you can put dry sheets to dust mop or wet sheets to mop the floor. There are dusting cloths that can be worn like a glove. There are sheets that act like a feather duster, but are easier to

FIGURE 8.1 Kitchen- and menu-related tasks for Judy.

Task	Short-Term Goal	Comment
Create menu plan	Judy will work with Mom each week (the day before grocery shopping) to create a menu plan for the following week.	By doing this with Mom, Judy will gain the needed skill.
Make grocery list	Judy will retrieve grocery list from refrigerator door with things that have been noted as needed from the store during the prior week. Judy and Mom will talk about recipes for things in menu plan and list things needed from the store for the recipes. Then Judy will practice checking on other items needed from the store. For example, is there enough milk? If not, she will write "milk" on the list.	
Grocery shopping	Judy and Mom will go grocery shopping together each week.	
Put away groceries	Upon coming home with the groceries, Judy and Mom will put them away together. Judy will be taught how to prepare vegetables, etc., for the refrigerator.	
Cooking simple meals	Judy will learn to cook meals (preferably ones from the menu plan she has learned how to prepare).	Initially, this will be done together with Mom, but gradually Mom's assistance will be reduced.

(continued)

FIGURE 8.1   (*Continued*)

Task	Short-Term Goal	Comment
Empty dishwasher	Judy will unload the dish-washer after breakfast every morning	Judy is able to do this skill fairly independently now. Mom and Judy can do this activity together rather than in a teaching phase.
Reload dishwasher	Judy will load the dish-washer after breakfast and add more after meals until ready to run.	Judy is able to do this skill fairly independently now. It can be done with Mom.

handle. Some have extensions for getting cobwebs out of the corners or off ceilings.

Someone in a wheelchair who is unable to handle a large mop and pail might be able to use the mops with disposable sheets to clean small areas. Many of the new feather dusters with disposable sheets come with adjustable long handles. They are intended for cobwebs on the ceilings, but are perfect for someone using a wheelchair. The extensions make it easier for someone sitting in a wheelchair or using a walker to reach an end table when he might not be able to get close enough to the table in the wheelchair or walker.

If he experiences problems with a particular task, visit your local supermarket or department store and look at some of the new products. You may find a way of adapting the method for him. Billy Ray always seemed to have difficulty using a dustpan. I tried a long-handled dustpan and various suggestions, but he still couldn't seem to get all the dirt swept up. It may be due to his low vision. Nevertheless, recently I was requested to evaluate some Swiffer® products and then review them on my blog. They sent us a Swiffer Sweep Vac. It has the same flat surface where a disposable dusting sheet is placed, but it also has a small vacuum unit that picks up larger things that the dusting sheet doesn't pick up. Billy Ray can push the button and pick up things he would normally have to use the dustpan for. That solved the problem he was experiencing with dustpans. It is also cordless with a rechargeable battery, so Billy Ray doesn't have to fight the cord like he does with other vacuums.

You also need to consider safety factors, especially with household chores. For example, Billy Ray spent about six weeks in a respite care home once when I couldn't take care of him due to some personal issues. One of the residents, who appeared to be quite high functioning, got under the sink and began mixing cleaning products together after staff left the cupboard unlocked. Whether he was just trying to clean or conducting a science project, I'm not sure. Nevertheless, the house had to be evacuated and aired out for many hours. Apparently, the things he mixed could have caused an explosion.

There are multiple types of cleaning products that have disposable pads. You may not feel comfortable having your child deal with large bottles of various chemicals. If that's the case, you can get toilet-cleaning products that have a disposable pad with the cleanser in them. There are similar products for cleaning the tub or wiping surfaces, as well as for other basic chores. The disposables allow ease in performing a variety of chores and prevent the need for having too many chemicals that could be accidentally mixed up.

Talk to him about what he needs to learn if he wants to have his own apartment one day. Make a big deal of his new skills. Have him hone the skills by practice and learn to get into the routine he will need by doing it at home before he has his own home.

His standards for housekeeping need not be your standards. He may want things more in view than orderly in the cupboards the way you do. It could be a form of security for him. On the other hand, if you are a "messie" (like me), he may want things put away more than you do. Clutter may bother him. Obviously, you don't want him to live in filth, but allow him to establish a style that is most comfortable for him.

Some tasks that will be necessary for independence or semi-independence are going to be more complicated. For example, if he is on medication and wants to live independently, he is going to have to take it on schedule independently. He may be into the routine from years of following it—and it will be no problem. Billy Ray automatically knows he is to take pills with his meals. He reminds me if they are not sitting by his dinner plate. He couldn't dispense them for himself, but he would remember to take them. Having them dispensed by the pharmacy in those little bubble packs would work for him.

If your adult child would not be good at noticing the time and taking medications appropriately, you can set up some type of buzzer reminders. Create them long before the transition while you are able to assist. That way there is comfort and some assurance of the ability to manage the system.

The more practice before transition, the better. The mother of an older teenager commented that she realized her daughter loved toast and jelly every morning, and it was probably time to teach her daughter to make toast since she would be getting her own apartment in a couple of years. Given all the things more complicated than toast to teach, that time frame for preparation might be a little slow.

If he uses visuals, you may want to create activity visuals for the tasks. Even if you don't create visuals, it would be a good idea to write down each task and the steps that he does in each one. This will be important not only for his reference, but for skill trainers, job coaches, and other assistants if you are not available to discuss them. Additionally, if there is a change of job coach or in-home support staff, the information is documented for training someone down the road.

He will probably establish a routine for doing things with you. But having a written schedule of activities will be a good reminder for him. You could do it in a pretty binder and make it special for him. We will formulize his schedule in a later chapter. It will serve the additional purpose of being available for in-home support personnel.

Finding a Roommate

In the description for what Judy would consider her pursuit of happiness, she wanted to share a home with a roommate. If she is still in school or a vocational program, she may have a friend that she thinks she would enjoy sharing an apartment or a house with. Judy's parent(s) could set a short-term goal to have her spend time with her friend away from school or work so they could see how comfortable their relationship is in a less-structured setting.

Think about what you would expect from a roommate for your child. For example, do you want him or her to pay equal amounts of the living costs? If Judy would pay more but the roommate would be able to assist more (requiring less paid assistance), would you be comfortable with that? Determining attitudes in advance will avoid disappointments later.

If he doesn't have such a friend, set a short-term goal to talk to a county case manager or an advisor in his vocational program. Mention the need for a roommate to anyone you think might know of someone. It may be that others know someone with whom he may be compatible, with similar goals.

Don't wait until he is ready to move into an apartment to begin thinking of a roommate. The best roommate will likely be a good friend. Knowing someone from school or work experience is not necessarily the same as really knowing the person. If they are buddies, they will likely help each other with needs and generally enjoy each other's company.

If Judy has a school or work friend (we'll call her "Dana") she thinks might be a future roommate, short-term goals might look like this:

- Ask Dana's Mom (or her parents) to have lunch or coffee without Judy and Dana first. Discuss her feelings about trying to help the ladies establish a relationship that could lead to a roommate experience later. Does this interfere with planning for Dana?

- Assuming Dana's family is willing, have a dinner at home or a restaurant that would include both families to get acquainted.

- Determine common interests that Judy and Dana share. For example, bowling or going to a movie. Make plans to take Judy and Dana for outings on a regular basis—weekly or every other week, whatever works. After the first few times, maybe you and Dana's mom can alternate providing assistance.

- After a few weeks of doing activities together, invite Dana to spend an evening or afternoon in your home.

- Maybe Dana's family will be willing to let the ladies spend alternate time in their home as time goes on.

- As they seem comfortable together, overnight visits might begin.

You would use similar short-term goals once you identified a potential roommate through a case manager or friends, but you might move a little more slowly since they are not as familiar with each other in the beginning.

Spending time together will show if they are compatible. You will rather quickly see if there is conflict between them or if they seem to grow closer. Conflict is not necessarily a sign that it won't work. Some conflict can be normal; the type and degree of conflict will have to be evaluated.

It will also be clear if the families can work together. Billy Ray and I experienced a bit of imbalance between another family and us. I wasn't looking for a roommate but a friend for Billy Ray to do things with outside of school. He never really bonded with friends in school or children in our church, but there was one girl (we will call her "Susie") with whom he had been in school for several years and seemed to like.

We would invite Susie to go to a movie on Saturdays and maybe an ice cream parlor, the zoo, day trips to the beach, etc. Sometimes they would just do things at our house for the afternoon. Soon, we had several incidences when Susie's parents were not home when I arrived to drop her off. Other times they failed to pick her up at the agreed-upon time.

Shortly, I began to get calls from her mom wondering if they could drop Susie off so they could go and do things. Next, they asked to borrow money. They had some challenges, and the amounts were small. I did not decline in the beginning; however, when there were no repayments *and* requests for more money, I began saying no.

On one occasion I asked them if Billy Ray could visit them. They agreed, but afterwards said he was "too busy" for them and couldn't come back without me. I was surprised by that because Billy Ray and Susie seemed to behave so well together at my home.

Susie began to speak about when she and Billy Ray would get married. I told her that since she was 12 and he was only 11, it was a little soon to talk about getting married. It became clear that her parents were encouraging her. One day when her parents dropped Susie off, her mom asked about the rest of the house. To my total shock, she asked me if Susie and Billy Ray would get the house when they got married!

As stated, we weren't thinking about a roommate at that time, and friendships are important. I struggled with whether to continue a relationship that could cause severe disappointment for both down the road.

Eventually, Billy Ray became less interested in doing things on the weekends with Susie. By then, we had met his stepfather, who lived on a farm. Billy Ray preferred to spend time doing things with his stepfather on the weekends than going into town to see Susie. They were no longer in school together after we moved in with Larry, and the relationship gradually died.

If it becomes clear that living together would not work, it is possible that the friendship can continue without becoming roommates.

TEACHING YOUR ADULT CHILD TO BE A SELF-ADVOCATE

Learning to advocate for your child was probably a major challenge for you. The frustration you have experienced and temptation to blow up will likely be experienced by your adult child at some point. He may not understand why it can be so frustrating to get his wishes honored.

One way to teach him to become a self-advocate is to take him to any meetings you attend regarding care or planning for him. If he is still in school, take him to the IEP meetings so he has the experience relating in such settings.

You probably have a stack of written "Rights" from many prior meetings. They often come with notices of a meeting. If you don't have a copy available, ask for a copy from the appropriate person. Spend some time explaining what the rights mean to him before you attend the meeting. Go over meeting agenda items with him before the meeting and get his input.

Suggest that he watch you the first time or two rather than taking the lead. However, make it a point to let him give his opinion in the meeting whenever possible. This allows him to practice being heard and gain self-confidence in speaking for himself.

If you live near a chapter of People First, it would be great for the two of you to attend meetings and let him join the group. He will find lots of support there. He will undoubtedly make some important friendships as well as learn a lot from this group. Contact information for this organization is in Appendix F, and Appendix D is an article on becoming a self-advocate that you might discuss with him or copy for him to keep as a reminder.

CREATING SHORT-TERM GOALS FOR OTHER TYPES OF PLANS

Creating short-term goals for a transitional plan will be somewhat complicated. In a perfect world you would have a second home for him behind your house and transition him gradually, adding in-home support staff who would understand his needs well and stay with him for many years.

As long as parents are available, it might be difficult to get funding for round-the-clock staffing. Thus, the first goal regarding funding might be to take the transitional plan to a meeting with the county case manager or other authority. Ask for an estimate of how long it will take to fund the required services. And ask what you may be able to start with in the meantime. For example, you may be able to begin with one shift of in-home staff plus a consultant so that you can train at least part of the team.

Have documentation available, if possible, that will demonstrate the need for consistency in procedures as well as health issues. A list of behavior issues and triggers will help to demonstrate the importance of this. You can discuss the advanced care that will be required if this system is not created for him in the transition. It is possible there will be a desire to set the system up earlier rather than risk very expensive care in an advanced facility if out-of-control behavior results from failure to have a system that works for him.

If you are able to negotiate a budget for one shift per day of in-home staff and monthly visits from the consultant, short-term goals might look like the following. (Note these goals don't assume that Mom or Dad—i.e., the present primary caregivers—works outside the home. If that is happening, the goals would need to be adjusted because of scheduling.)

- Draft schedule including goals (training/activities) that he will work on from the transitional plan.
- Create or update any needed visuals or picture schedules.
- Prepare documentation explaining procedures and schedule. (In Chapter 11 we will discuss documentation, vital for plans like Zach's—that will be helpful to have on hand.)
- Begin working on the schedule and starting on the goals with him before having the consultant or staff come (if possible) so you can resolve any problem areas.
- Meet with available consultants and select one.
- Meet with the selected consultant and provide documentation as well as opportunities to spend time with your adult child and get to know him.
- Work with the consultant to select in-home staff.
- Train staff in procedures and schedule for your adult child.

The above short-term goals will get the transition started in your home. You can also create other goals based on the transition plan and prioritize in terms of when to do them. For example, if the case manager estimated that the availability of a service slot for funding is four years, you can ask the Housing Authority or other rent assistance programs in your area how long their waiting list is. Ask if you can put him on the waiting list now. And ask whether he'll remain on the list if he isn't ready when his name comes to the top.

You can create more goals, such as sharing information with the potential guardians and personal advocates so that they have a good understanding of his needs, as well as who he is as a person. Arrange as much contact as possible between him and those who will be involved in his adult life. He will be more comfortable with them when they need to take a greater role in his life, and they will be more familiar with him.

Referring back to the plans in Chapter 7, the goals for Denny will have some similarity to Zach's, but will be fewer. Denny will remain at home while waiting for a placement. He will have in-home support staff while his parents are at work. Denny and his staff will need a schedule for staff training. And, like Zach, Denny's future guardian and personal advocate will need to have a good understanding of Denny and his needs.

Additionally, you could check with the case manager at the facility where you're planning to place Denny. Ask if the facility takes residents to community events (such as dances) regularly or hosts events where others are invited to the facility. It may be possible to have Denny attend those events before his placement to establish friendships with potential fellow residents and staff. By inquiring about the kinds of things Denny would be allowed to have in his room, you can get a jump on collecting items he'll be comfortable with—and he'll have them right away when he moves there.

If Denny enjoys going to church but his present congregation is too far from the facility where he'll be, you and Denny could occasionally visit a church nearer the facility. This would allow him to have existing relationships at the time he transitions to that community.

You and Denny might also visit the surrounding community from time to time. This would enable him to become familiar with restaurants, stores, and recreational facilities that he might frequent in the future. There would be less new about his community when he moves there.

Continue setting short-term goals for each transition (long-term) goal until finished. Prioritize which ones you and your child will work on first.

9

ESTATE PLANNING

SOMETHING WE GOTTA DO SOMEDAY

Estate planning is something that we think about and plan to do but unfortunately may leave to the last minute. I have heard multiple stories of adult children still living at home with parents who die suddenly or become disabled. Sometimes they have never written a last will and testament or nominated guardians—no arrangements have been made for an adult child who is unable to care for herself. Sometimes this is because of financial concerns or just too many day-to-day details to deal with. We don't expect to die, and we may hope to survive a child with disabilities.

To be honest, it is morbid and scary to think about it. Realistically, it is like leaving an adult with special needs unprotected from a multitude of harms. Lack of planning will make an already difficult situation much more painful for your adult child.

A PLAN TAKES MORE THAN A WILL OR TRUST

I have heard parents talk as if they had their adult child fully protected in the event of their death merely by writing a will. If only that were true; but in fact, it usually is not. Wills and trusts generally are financial instruments that also nominate representatives for your child[ren]. Those documents are very important, but they need to be supplemented with other documents.

It is also important for representatives and caregivers to have a good understanding of your adult child's special needs, day to day, medical history, family history, and other details that are not covered by estate-planning documents. This is true regardless of how independent she will be. The trustee, for example, will need to understand medical costs and other information in order to budget funds and distributions for her in a prudent way.

The reality is that estate-planning documents can't possibly contain all the necessary information and the important history to provide for her care. In fact, it isn't a good idea to put personal information in a will or trust that might be filed at the court and available publicly. I strongly suggest that you supplement your estate-planning documents with additional information relative to your adult child's needs, care, history, and goals.

If you have read my other writing or blogs or heard me speak, you probably know that when I was a fiduciary (guardian/conservator/trustee), I dealt with many parents' wills or trusts that said something like "to enable my child to maintain the same standard of living she maintained during my lifetime." What does that mean in terms of how to care for a child or adult child? If the named guardian or caregiver has not been around the child, he or she may not have a clue about who the child is as a person—or what her special needs are. This person may not have the answers to important questions such as:

- What is the general health of the person? Is special medical care needed? Allergies?
- Who are her medical providers and dentist? Where are they located? How often does she need to visit them?
- What kinds of foods does she eat? This would include what she will tolerate as well as any food allergies.
- What kind of assistance does she require?

- What kind of lifestyle is she most comfortable with?
- What is her weekly schedule?
- Who are her friends and significant people in her life? How do I reach them?
- Is there a funeral trust for the adult child with your family arrangements or elsewhere?

The idea of supplementing estate-planning documents is to answer questions about your adult child that may not be obvious from those documents. Your adult child may be able to function fairly independently, but you still may monitor certain things fairly closely during your lifetime; and these things might not be obvious to others. She may have trouble communicating small needs for assistance. She may be embarrassed or depressed from grief of your absence. Whatever the situation, having a supplemental file will make a big difference in assuring things go better for her after you are no longer able to monitor her care and protection.

For someone who lives reasonably independently, you might write something like this:

Jeremy is able to care of himself quite well. We assist him with:

- Calling the transportation company when he needs to change his pickup time. Sometimes he can do this, but other times the long wait and confusing voice mail options frustrate him and he can be stuck for the rest of the day because he didn't get through to make the changes.
- Hiring housekeeping and yard work assistants.
  - Jeremy keeps up with day-to-day cleaning and household chores on his own, but he has difficulty dusting the cobwebs in the ceiling and pulling out the furniture to clean under it. We arrange for someone to come in about every four months to do spring-cleaning-type chores.
  - He likes to putter in the flowerbeds—pulling weeds and planting flowers—and he waters the yard faithfully. In the storage shed is a stool that he sits on when working in the flower beds.
  - Each spring we make an outing of going to the nursery for him to choose flowers he wants to plant, and then we have lunch. Sometimes it might take him a week to get them all in the

ground. He will work on them after work and then stop when
it gets dark or he gets tired. He continues the process each
night until it's finished.

○ The lawnmower is too much for him. We have subscribed to a
lawnmowing service for his grass.

Jeremy works at Sally's restaurant as a dishwasher and cook's
helper. He loves the staff and the customers there. He bonds to his co-
workers, so he feels the loss deeply when someone quits. The manager
calls me when someone quits, and I visit Jeremy to discuss that his co-
worker is leaving. He will be sad, but able to handle it if he is prepared.

Paydays are on the 12th and 27th of each month. Jeremy was
robbed once after going to the bank. He is frightened to do it again.
His boss frequently takes him to the bank and then home on paydays.
If he can't do it, I pick him up and take him to the bank.

You could include a copy of Jeremy's medical history with a list of medications and the names and addresses of his doctor, pharmacy, and dentist,
and a copy of the transitional plan with the roles of anyone else involved in
his life, edited to include any changes that have been made.

If you create the documents recommended in *Parenting Your Complex
Child* (history, visuals including pictures schedules, medication list, journal,
summaries, and care manual) for someone with more complex needs, they
can easily be combined into a section of your planning notebook or in a
separate notebook. If you are not creating the documents, you will find numerous types of care manuals available from organizations or agencies and
on the Internet. Depending on the complexities of your adult child, such
documents may be more than adequate.

If she is nonverbal or has difficulty communicating, others may not be
able to anticipate her needs in the way that is natural to you. Being more
specific is necessary.

In Chapter 16 of *Parenting Your Complex Child*, I talked about an estate-
planning file that will work in this case too: "The communication and documentation systems suggested in this book [*Parenting Your Complex Child*]
will teach someone to take care of your child if you are hit by a car."[20] As I
was finishing this chapter, I thought about the parents of the clients that I
worked with. Many of the parents' estate plans made provisions "to enable
him to maintain the same standard of living he enjoyed during my lifetime." What does that mean? Take him out for dinner at a favorite buffet? If
so, what were his favorite foods? In many cases, the child can't communi-

cate that to his or her new guardian. I once created an activity visual for Billy Ray to understand the steps in going to a buffet restaurant. It also has a list of his favorite foods, so that anyone taking him to that buffet would know what he normally likes. These types of visuals that you create for your child's present use are great tools for an estate-planning file as well.

"As you are working to make your child's life as meaningful as possible, be reassured that the documentation you use for her today is also preparing for the future."[21] In Chapter 11 we will talk more about documenting day-to-day care for someone who requires support staff or other assistance. Many of those documents are also appropriate for your estate-planning file.

REPRESENTATIVES TO ACT FOR YOUR ESTATE AND FOR YOUR CHILD(REN)

Each state has its own rules about fiduciaries (someone who acts for another person). The information presented here may not be exactly the same as in your area. It is intended to give you a basic idea of the responsibilities. But you will need to check with your attorney about the laws where you are.

Guardian (Sometimes Referred to as Guardian of the Person)

After the manuscript for *Parenting Your Complex Child* had already been submitted to my publisher, Billy Ray experienced a major health crisis. He had two surgeries in 47 hours. After the second one, he didn't resume breathing as he should. This created all kinds of issues for us to deal with because I had not acquired guardianship for him. My editor suggested that we add the following about guardianship to help other parents avoid a similar situation:

> Guardianship can best be explained by comparing it to parenting. Parents are effectively the child's guardians by birth or adoption. Parents are responsible for making medical, educational, and life decisions for their children when the children are too young to make competent choices or take care of themselves. When a child becomes legally an adult, she is able to make her own decisions. That means that you can no longer make educational or medical decisions for her.
>
> In the case of a disabled person who becomes an adult but is not able to assume responsibility for himself, the parent must show the

court that he is unable to make competent medical and other care decisions without the protection of a guardian. Effectively, you ask the
court to extend your ability to care for your child by becoming his legal
guardian.

It is easy to go with the flow and not deal with this issue. If you
haven't changed doctors, most doctors continue to treat your child
with your consent as always. When an emergency arises, things can
change rapidly. For example, after Billy Ray's emergency room crisis,
he ended up on the ventilator for nine days. In order for the ventilator
to be removed at my request, guardianship would have to be established. Fortunately, it didn't come to that point, but it is an important
thing to remember.[22]

Sometimes doctors and other professionals will accept the consent of
the parent long after the child attains legal age. This is especially true if the
professional has known the family for many years. However, legally these
professionals do not have to honor your wishes unless you're a guardian.

Not everyone with disabilities needs a guardian. The deciding factor
will be her ability to understand the information provided by a professional
and make reasonable decisions relative to her care and safety. In some areas
there are also limited guardianships that provide authority to act in a more
limited way.

Depending on the assets of an adult with disabilities and the laws in
your area, the guardian may also handle financial matters. For example, if
the law in your area sets a limit of $10,000 in assets, and the adult has less
than that, the guardian will also be able to manage the monies and financial matters for the person.

Conservator (Sometimes Called Guardian of the Estate)

A conservator manages financial matters but cannot make medical decisions
or life decisions. For example, a conservator may obtain health insurance
but doesn't have the authority to consent to treatment. He or she may sign
a lease on an apartment and pay the bills out of the person's funds.

Some adults with disabilities need a conservator to help with financial
matters, but do not require a guardian. Others require both. Still others are
able to pay their own bills and generally manage their own funds with help
from a family member or accountant, without the need of a court-appointed
conservator.

Trustee

If parents or grandparents leave a bequest to a child who is unable to man-age her own financial affairs—or for some reason can't receive larger amounts of assets—they may put it in a testamentary (contained in a will) trust or some form of living trust. In the will or trust, the trustor (person owning the property—parents, grandparents, etc.) appoints the trustee to manage those funds. It is a different role than a conservator because trustees are not ap-pointed to manage the person's entire estate, only specific conditions con-tained in the trust. A conservator, on the other hand, manages a person's personal funds including government benefits outside the trust.

There are many types of special needs trusts, but for the purpose of this chapter I only want to give you an idea how they work. You will need to get legal advice about the type of trust that is appropriate in your case.

For example, perhaps your adult child receives Supplemental Security Income, Medicaid, and other governmental benefits. There are generally limits to the amount of assets, including cash savings and property, a person can have and still receive services. For example, for Medicaid, a person can't have more than $2,000 in cash and assets. Usually, a home and car are excluded from that limit. A special needs trust can receive the assets and coordinate with regulations to provide only monies and care not covered by the governmental programs. This will protect the eligibility for services.

If she works and lives independently, but gets reduced rent or food stamps, this can be affected by change in assets or income from an inheri-tance as well. A trust could provide supplemental needs without jeopardiz-ing the benefits.

If she is in a residential facility funded by Medicaid or other govern-ment funding, she may only be allowed to keep a very small monthly al-lowance out of her SSI or other income and must contribute the balance as her share. The difference will be picked up by the government funding. However, there may be specific services and items that are not covered by Medicaid such as the following:

- Certain medical treatments and medications. For example, if the doctor prescribes a medication that is not covered by insurance, it is possible that the trust could pay for it, if the trust is written to provide for that.

- Specialized clothing. Generally, clothing must come out of the small monthly allowance. If she requires a lot of clothes because of incontinency or behavior that destroys her clothes, the trust could provide extra clothing.

- Certain medical equipment that is not covered by Medicaid or other insurance.

- Furniture and other personal needs not provided for by Medicaid and/or too expensive to be purchased out of the allowance.

- Some types of educational or vocational training.

- Vacations and recreation. The trust can provide things that are not covered by the funding source and will not make a person ineligible for services. This could include the cost of having a staff person accompany the person on vacation, even though the camp or other vacation is paid for through a government program.

Additionally, if the law in your area allows special needs trusts to supplement uncovered needs, you will be better off putting funds into trust so that it will pay for years of supplemental things, rather than having to do a short-term spend-down of funds and then not be able to meet extraordinary needs that are not covered by government assistance.

Another possibility may be that your adult child is still at home with you at the time of your death. She may qualify for services to bring help into the home. In some areas you could leave your home to her in your will. In other areas, it would disqualify her for governmental services. However, it is possible that a trust could actually own the house and under whatever laws or regulations that apply, she could live there rent free or at a reduced rent.

Most parents of a child with special needs have had high expenses and high care needs while the child is at home. That can strongly impact what is left at the death of the parent(s). You may think that you don't have significant monies to worry about a trust. That is something to think about cautiously and research carefully. For example, if you have a small insurance policy on your life, it could put your adult child over the limit, disqualifying her for Medicaid or other governmental funding. Some areas may allow her to do a spend-down where she would use it up and then be restarted on the program after her assets are below the allowable asset limit. Other areas would require that she go back on the waiting list for services when her assets go below that level. That could be a complicated situation for her.

Even if your adult child is not on government assistance, it may be desirable to put assets in a trust if you have concerns that they would be used up too fast and not be available for later needs.

OTHER CONSIDERATIONS

You may want to request provisions in your estate-planning documents that are not necessary in other people's documents. For example, I hope that the granddaughter I mentioned, or other grandchildren, will maintain relationships with Billy Ray and maintain his story. This granddaughter lives in a nearby state now and will be going away for college. Visiting Billy Ray regularly will cost her too much. But a provision in a special needs trust can easily provide for reimbursement of those expenses to enable regular visits.

There will be things that your adult child needs that may not be clear to the nominated representative and are not covered by funding outside a trust. For example, Billy Ray does a lot of bouncing on his bed, which breaks the box springs regularly. Neither Medicaid nor his county funding would provide replacements. A note to the nominated representative or a provision in the trust would warn of this need.

If there are siblings, you will need to think through taking care of your adult child with special needs while still being fair to your other children or grandchildren. The more you think through the issues before visiting your attorney, the fewer "billable hours" you will run up. You will still want to discuss the issues with your attorney, but you'll have a basic idea of what you want to accomplish beforehand.

There may be someone in your circle of friends and family whom you specifically do not want to serve as guardian, conservator, or trustee. Maybe decisions he or she has made about the care of his or her own children or the way he or she has managed funds concerns you, and you wouldn't be comfortable with this person's abilities to make prudent decisions for your adult child. Tell your attorney and ask how to document that. Your attorney may want you to write a letter to that effect and have it notarized. Thus, your wishes will be known when you are not available to state them.

In trying to ascertain what you want included in your estate-planning documents, also consider things that are important for your nominee to understand about care and support to your adult child. Perhaps the nominated guardian will not actually have your child living in his or her home but still needs to have a thorough understanding of care requirements to be able to advocate for her.

10

WORKING WITH
YOUR ATTORNEY

THE IMPORTANCE OF THE RELATIONSHIP BETWEEN
YOU AND YOUR ATTORNEY

Attorneys may have a reputation for being expensive and difficult to deal with, but that is not necessarily accurate. As in any profession, there are some people you'll relate to better than others. The legal field is no exception. And, in fact, an attorney who will take time to understand your wishes and your adult child's needs can become an important ally. Not only will he give you legal advice but you can count on him to follow up with the appointment of fiduciaries you choose to act for your child and to help them advocate for your child in the event of problems with carrying out the plan.

As I've recommended regarding doctors, if you can't relate to one and she won't listen to you, choose another one. The same applies to attorneys. You will need the attorney to have a greater understanding of your family situation than some families may require. Thus, the relationship needs to work well to enhance that understanding.

As with choosing any other professional, you won't learn much about a person from a yellow pages listing. It's better, if possible, to get a referral from friends or family members who have used that attorney. Additionally, some agencies have lists of attorneys who have been helpful to their clients. Some attorneys will speak at support groups and you may get a chance to hear them before scheduling an appointment.

Billy Ray has taught me a lot about people by the way they respond to him. If they are uncomfortable or less than polite with him, I am not comfortable working with them. I like to take him with me at the beginning of an appointment. I don't necessarily take him in for the appointment when I am going to discuss things that I know will confuse or upset him; I might take a support staff person or a friend along. That way Billy Ray gets a chance to meet the attorney and vice versa then perhaps goes out with a friend during the appointment.

SOME TIPS FOR WORKING WITH AN ATTORNEY

Lawyers can be expensive, and, given all the costs of taking care of your child, that can be a challenge. However, there are options:

- Many attorneys will handle certain cases *pro bono* (without charge) or at a reduced rate. Some do not charge for the first visit. When you go to that visit, be up front about what you can afford and see if you can negotiate something affordable for you.
- Depending on where you live, there may be legal clinics that are free or discounted based on income. An added advantage of this is that there may be a young attorney starting out by working in the legal clinic. Later he may start his own practice and take some of his special clients along at a reduced rate.

One of the best ways to reduce the cost is to prepare for the visits. If the attorney sends forms to complete, be sure to complete them and bring them to the appointment. If you don't get such forms, you can create a sheet with basic information such as:

- Name and spouse's name (if any), address, phone number.
- Children, including stepchildren, and their ages.
- Disability of your child(ren) and brief statement about future planning needs.
  - Be sure to include any governmental benefits that your child(ren) receive; estate plans must take those into consideration so that the plan itself won't disqualify your child from receiving services.
- Financial information (your assets, property, income, extraordinary expenses).

As stated, a plan for your child is more involved than a standard estate-planning document. However, you will want your attorney to be somewhat aware of the plan because he can assist or provide information to others when you can't be available to do that.

As stated in Chapter 16, *Parenting Your Complex Child*:

I have seen estate planning documents specify that the same standard of living the child received in the parent's lifetime should be maintained, but then fail to demonstrate what that standard is. If the professional or distant friend or family member designated to act on behalf of the child did not have a high degree of communication with you and your child, he or she may not have a clear understanding of what that standard of living was. Sometimes parents have not provided the child's chosen representative with this kind of information because they have died suddenly or they suffer from a physical condition, such as dementia. Key issues such as medical history and even funeral planning for the child are not always known to your child's representative after you are no longer available.[23]

If you create an estate-planning file or notebook, it would be a good idea to take it with you sometime when you visit your attorney. Obviously, you don't want to spend a lot of billable hours on it, and the file doesn't need to be left with the attorney. However, having a look at a day in your adult child's picture schedule, for example, could make a big difference in the attorney's ability to better understand him and his needs as the estate-planning documents are being written.

In my previous book, I suggested revising yearly the Abbreviated Chronological History, preferably near a child's birthday, and communicating with the representatives nominated in your estate-planning documents to represent your child. It is a good idea to copy in the attorney, who may or may not need to spend a lot of time on the annual review, but the information will be available in his or her file when needed by your adult child's representative. And the annual update may remind the attorney about some new law or government regulation that he wanted you to know about. Perhaps you need to change some provision of your estate-planning documents.

Sometimes sending a letter with the updated history to the nominated representatives will cause them to rethink their willingness to serve. Disappointing as that may be, it is better to know while you are still available to choose a replacement.

Other times, the letter and history will bring to mind questions that the representative may want to ask you. This gives you a chance to provide information that you may not have thought about sharing earlier.

Ask your attorney how often you need to come back for revisions to your estate-planning documents. Some attorneys will recommend yearly or every-other-year visits. Others may say every five years is enough. You can negotiate the frequency. Also, ask what kinds of things would require a change in your estate-planning documents. That way you will understand when you should come back, beyond the regular visits you negotiated with the attorney.

Your attorney will be one of the best protections for your adult child. If you take the time to find an attorney whom you can relate to and provide some opportunity for the attorney to understand your adult child's needs, he can be your voice for your child when you can't be there.

CHAPTER

11

IMPLEMENTING THE PLAN
A STEP AT A TIME

RECLAIMING THE WAIT TIME

If you have worked through creating a transitional plan and short-term goals, you wonder what to do now. Maybe your adult child is still on a waiting list for a vocational and/or residential program. While you wait, you can work on some of the short-term goals. And you can put the waiting time to good use by working on training and by maintaining relationships that you have helped him establish.

Work on allowing as much independence in tasks and visiting friends as possible. If his goal is to live independently in an apartment and you have determined that he is capable of that, he is going to have to spend time alone in his new apartment. Maybe you have been very protective, never leaving him alone in the house. You don't want that to begin the first day he moves into his apartment. That would be too scary for him. So, begin to allow him to remain at home alone for very short time periods. A few short minutes the first time will be less heart wrenching for both of you. If you come back and find the house still standing and he is busy doing some reasonable activity, try it again soon—this time for longer. If he seems terrified and/or something has gone wrong, discuss it with him. Was he frightened? Reassure him and try to work through his concerns.

Training on locking doors and windows is important, but should be done so as not to add fear. A good way to do that is by modeling the behavior at other times, such as when you are leaving the house. Then, you can say, "Be sure to lock the door" when you leave your adult child alone and not make a big deal of it.

The fear of being alone is not unique to someone with disabilities. I remember how excited and terrified I was the first time I was alone in my own apartment. He may really want to have his own space and his own home, but still experience fear. Try to help him adjust to it little by little with practice. He will likely adjust. And if not, it is better to know now, so you can modify the plan.

Check in regularly with the case manager or agency personnel to determine where his name is on the waiting list. This will help you know how to work through goals in the meantime and keep you and your adult child prepared.

ACCUMULATING THINGS FOR THE NEW HOME

Think about the furniture and other household items he will need in his apartment. Depending on your ability to store things, you could visit local thrift stores or secondhand stores together. Accumulating things a little at a time will help him understand that you are preparing for his adult life despite the wait for it to happen.

You might consider if there are a few pieces of furniture or other items at home that you could get by without or replace. That way he will have more of a sense of home in his new home. If it will be necessary to save money for new furniture, talk to him about not being able to do some things that cost money so that you can save for his new furniture. Look at catalogs or online stores and make a list together about what he will need.

Look at the furniture and bedding in his room. Maybe it is good enough to keep for when he comes home for a weekend, but not good enough for him to take to his own apartment. The initial insecurity he faces moving into his own home could be exacerbated by totally new surroundings. While you are waiting for the transition, maybe you can replace one piece of his bedroom furniture. That way he gets used to using it before moving with it to his own home. If possible, put the prior things in storage to restore his room in your home after he moves. That way he will have things he is comfortable with in his new home and at your home.

If the plan is for him to go to some sort of group setting, attempt to find out what kinds of things he will be able to take with him. The more you pick up a piece at a time, the easier it will be on you when he arrives at the top of the list for a vacancy.

Planning for transition items should include clothing replacement and discarding things that he won't wear. That may be more difficult than you think. Billy Ray has many items that he will not wear but insists on keeping. Getting rid of them is a major challenge especially since he does notice. For example, he has a blue shirt that he won't wear, but he uses it as a marker for where he wants to hang other clothes. If I tried to sneak it out of his closet, it would not be a fun time. He loves to go shopping and would pick out a whole new wardrobe if I let him, but he would not always wear the new things after we got them home, even though he had selected them. If you have issues like this, the earlier you start with wardrobe replacements, the easier it is going to be once transition happens.

CREATING AND PREPARING A SCHEDULE

If you haven't already done so, this is a good time to begin to create a schedule for him to work on short-term goals and train in new tasks, for example, doing his laundry on specific day(s) and scheduling other activities throughout the week. Put it in any format that he will find acceptable or easy to use. The easier it is for him to use, the more likely he will follow the schedule later.

I have used picture schedules for Billy Ray that include activities and tasks. For more involved tasks, I do activity visuals geared to one specific activity, not the entire schedule. You can see samples of picture schedules on my website, www.parentingyourcomplexchild.com. I used the homemade picture schedules for him because even though he is mostly verbal, there are times when he responds better to visual cues. It also helps his support staff learn the routine. The picture schedules are used in my training manual as well as for Billy Ray's personal schedule notebook.

Recently, I received a demo copy of software called Picture Planner, created by Eugene Research (www.eugeneresearch.org). Picture Planner—which should be on the market by the time this book is available—enables you to upload your own digital pictures and create activities or task schedules easily. It is much simpler to create than my homemade picture schedules and works pretty well for my son.

Ideally, the schedule you work out together and the format he uses while waiting for transition can go with him right into his transition. He can likely still do laundry on Wednesdays if he wants to; that may add security to his new home. If he is using a planner such as Picture Planner, it will be fairly easy to change it to his new schedule once he has moved and feels more comfortable. If he has some computer skills, you may even be able to help him learn to create his own planner using Picture Planner. Once the pictures are loaded, it is a fairly simple process to create a schedule.

Depending on his preferences and need for visuals, you could also create a combination planner and chore list system. At one point after Billy Ray got comfortable with his schedule, we reduced the entries and just put "household chores" during the time allotted for that. Then we created chore lists using Chore Genie (Weco Software, www.wecosoft.com). Chore Genie organizes each task by day and time (morning, afternoon, or evening) to be done. You can print out the list of chores for a specific day. It even comes with a place to check off each chore. Billy Ray enjoys checking off tasks that he has completed, so it works well for him. Your adult child may prefer some other kind of system. As always, do what works for him.

CREATING A TRAINING MANUAL

One important consideration in reviewing the options is whether your child would be able to say, "this is not working" if something is bothering him. Work with his advocate or case manager to understand any hints that he may give in terms of behavior (including meltdowns or withdrawal). You may also want to write it down for reference when you aren't available.

I have spoken with several parents who have worked to help their adult child transition into adult situations of some kind. Several have made the comment that it is all arranged only to fall apart because staff depart or programs change. The nagging question of what if that happens after parents are unavailable recurs. That is because, as stated, the involvement of the parent(s) is never really over until it is impossible to go on.

If you develop a training manual, you will be able to continue "training" staff long after you are no longer able to physically train them. Create this training manual even if you are not hiring assistance for him right now. It contains information needed to train someone to assist him to the degree he requires it. Additionally, it is an introduction to him as a person. You can explain approaches that work best, triggers to avoid, medical issues to monitor, and other important facts.

It might seem unnecessary to do this if your adult child is fairly independent and needs little assistance. However, there are probably more things that you do to support him than you realize. There may also be things in the past that could become important down the road that he will be unwilling to talk about.

For someone who lives independently with little assistance you might include only a short summary similar to the one we did for Jeremy in Chapter 9. Judy might require slightly more documentation than Jeremy because she receives more assistance. Zach and Denny, on the other hand, will require a substantially more detailed training manual because they require substantially more assistance in their daily lives than either Judy or Jeremy.

You won't need to tell his whole story because you did that for him to have and for others to preserve in the event of loss. However, the story is not a training manual. The story is something that he can enjoy looking at and sharing. The training manual is intended to provide information about his needs that you may or may not share with him, but that others will need to know.

What you put in the training manual will depend on his needs. Here are some ideas:

- A simple introduction. Include clues such as—
  - His personality. What makes him happy and what makes him sad.
  - What is important to him.
    - Maybe a special friendship that he enjoys or his service dog or anything else that is significant to him.
    - Having things in his closet or room a certain way.

- The process he must go through to select his clothes (or other tasks) especially if it might appear somewhat illogical to others but would confuse him or cause a meltdown if he's not allowed to do in his own way.
- Anything else unique to him, and especially important or likely to trigger issues? For example,
  - Does it upset him to go to noisy environments? And how is it handled when unavoidable?
  - Do fluorescent lights set him off?
  - Any other triggers that consistently create confusion or behavior issues?
- Does he have a need for special care?
  - Depending on the type of care, I do "protocols" such as:
    - Health Protocol: Include medical conditions that require special care at home, appointments with the doctor or lab, diets, or medications.
    - Safety Protocol: Include things such as:
      - Is it safe for him to be outside in the yard alone or take a walk on his own?
      - What's the safe distance between him and staff when out in public (next to him or close enough for visual contact or earshot only, etc.)?
- A week in his life:
  - You could include his schedule in whatever format you created it. Usually, a week is enough to give someone the routine. But if he has twice-monthly activities, for example, you may use a different time period.
  - Include notes about things that might not appear in the schedule, such as:
    - He has a ritual of saying goodnight to his service dog, but he doesn't want her on his bed. He is most secure if she sleeps on the floor between his dresser and his bed where he can reach out and touch her during the night if he wishes.
    - He sleeps with a movie on repeat so it continues to play throughout the night. When he goes to sleep, I turn the volume down pretty low, but he does want it on if he wakes up.

- Procedures that are important to him:
  - If he needs to do things certain ways, include instructions on how to assist and when to let him do things on his own. For example, he makes his own bed and staff should not straighten it—even if it is not made to their personal standards. On the other hand, he may need help with certain tasks.
  - Does he need to have the furniture a certain way to make him feel secure? (Note: This might seem silly, but some well-meaning staff have come in and rearranged someone's room or home to make it look "nicer" only to upset or confuse the person. You need to be specific.)
- Communication by behavior:
  - Are there certain things that will trigger undesirable behavior, but may not be obvious to someone who doesn't know him well yet? For example, if he is ill, he may communicate that by certain sounds or aggressive behavior. That should be noted.

When I write care or training manuals for Billy Ray's support staff, the questions they ask and issues that arise tend to trigger my memory about other things that should be included. Additionally, when there is a change of staff, sometimes I realize that the former staff member and I made a change in procedure or schedule, but didn't note it in the manual. That will trigger a revision. The manual will be a work in progress for quite a while. It will be helpful if it can be maintained on a computer file so changes can be made more easily.

If you are not ready to revise the manual itself, but a change occurs, it is always a good idea to make handwritten notes in the appropriate spot of the manual. That way the information is not forgotten when the manual is revised. It will be there for others working with him.

I don't recommend allowing support staff to take the manual home. Frequently, they see it as their personal possession; they even take it home without mentioning it. Some will say that they don't have time to read it when they are with your adult child. But all too often, when they take it home with them it doesn't come back, and it appears that they don't read it at home anyway. Even if the manual is on computer, it takes time and expense to recreate it. Additionally, there are confidentiality issues because it may contain personal information that you want to stay within your adult child's home.

FINALIZING THE TRANSITION PLAN AND SHORT-TERM GOALS

After you have been working on the short-term goals, it is a good time to take another look at the transition plan and the long-term goals. As you look at it, consider how it is working by asking yourself questions such as the following:

- Based on what you have learned, either by research or training thus far, does it still seem likely he will be able to accomplish the plan?
- Is there anything that could be done to make goals easier or more achievable for him?
- Should the plan be somewhat modified without destroying his dream?
- Is there more of the plan that could be started while waiting for services?

There can be many things that would cause you to take another look at the plan—a longer-than-expected waiting time for a service slot, for example. Or he may have approval for funding for part of the plan but not all of it. Explore with the case manager what could be done to modify the plan so that he could begin transition, at least in part.

Sometimes there are opportunities that might not be known without raising the issue one more time or exploring the options further. For example, he wants his own apartment, but funding for full-time support staff and a reduced rent apartment is not available. Maybe the case manager is aware of an apartment program where a block of apartments is supervised by assistants. Each one might be shared with one or more roommates. Perhaps the funding gap could be bridged with funds from a different program.

As stated in Chapter 1, it is not unusual for adult children to remain home until their parents are quite elderly, become ill, or even pass away. That's why keeping the training manual and estate-planning file up to date should be a priority. It may seem to you as though it will never happen; it may seem too far off to deal with. But the fact is, transition will happen with or without your assistance. That's why you should have as much documentation as possible available for when the time comes.

Most important: Don't just let years go by without staying in touch with the local agency. It is entirely possible that the case manager has every intention of checking in with you, but due to her workload she'll let it slip.

Your contact will ensure that things are reviewed periodically. That doesn't mean you should call every week just to check in. Quarterly contact is reasonable. A quick email or telephone call is usually enough to jog her memory and get her to take another look at planning for your child.

Another important point that should be discussed is allowing him as much independence as possible and/or focusing some of his dependence on others instead of you. I am not saying you must separate from him emotionally. You will always be Mom, Dad, Grandma, or whoever you are to him. The loving relationship you maintain with him is important. However, the less *dependent* he is on you for his every need, the less traumatic the physical separation of transition will be on him.

Many times the county or another government agency will provide some services while you are waiting for additional services. For example, maybe you'll get an aide to do some activities with him each week, or an aide to help you with activities such as bathing him as it gets more difficult for you to assist him. Exploring all those potentials with the case manager will help you. And it will help him to be less dependent on you.

CHAPTER 12

THE NEST MAY SEEM EMPTY, BUT YOU AREN'T DONE YET

FIRST, THE UNEXPECTED SADNESS

You and your adult child have worked hard, dreaming of the day when she would be transitioned into what will become her adult life. You expected it to be a joyous time, and it is. However, it is also a sad time for both of you because it is a separation that cuts deeper than you could have imagined.

When Billy Ray was 17 years old, we placed him in a treatment center for the purpose of restructuring his medications. The pain for both of us was literally devastating. I only made it one block before I had to pull over because I was crying hysterically (this from someone who doesn't usually cry). Billy Ray was having a similar reaction at the facility. I remember saying to the case manager that I wanted him to go to his adult placement after this temporary placement because I didn't want either of us to go through this trauma again. That didn't happen, but it seemed easier at the time.

Some group homes and other programs want you to delay the first visit until your child is settled in. That might be as long as a month. While that logic may seem understandable, it can also be devastating to the person and her family. You know your adult child better than anyone else. If you feel that it is too much for her to bear, advocate strongly to have some kind of contact—even if it is by phone—so that her security is not so threatened that it jeopardizes her chance to succeed in her new living situation. Talk to her about the program rules. Say that you will visit as soon as you are allowed and that she can call you any time she needs you. Assure her that she is allowed to do that.

Don't worry about bothering program staff. Even if a visit is not planned, check on her often by phone in the beginning. If problems arise, you want to be aware of them so you can advocate and assist with solutions.

Parents who have moved their adult children into their own apartment have shared that while they understood the children needed to be released from the nest and allowed to fly as free as possible, the kicked-in-the-stomach feeling when they closed the apartment door for the first time was almost unbearable.

Prepare yourself and your adult child for this sadness and recognize together that your relationship will continue, but in a somewhat different way. Eventually, she will feel the pride in having less dependence on you, but it will take time for both of you.

To the degree possible, don't let her know how hard it is on you. If she expresses her sadness, you can identify with it; however, if she is adjusting well, you don't want to share your sadness. That could make her feel guilty.

YOUR JOB GOES ON

As we said in Chapter 1, you may get the extra bedroom, but the nest in your heart is never empty. It can actually be harder for you as a parent to deal with the transition than to have your adult child in the nest where you know she is safe.

There will need to be a balance between preparing her to get along with less of your involvement and ensuring she is safe and happy. Overprotection is natural. On the other hand, reality speaks deep in your heart that you won't always be able to be there for her as much as you are today. Tapering off gradually will be less stressful for her than sudden loss when you just can't do as much.

If she is in her own apartment, you will probably want to check in daily to ensure that she is eating appropriately, taking medications (if any), keeping the apartment clean, and maintaining her schedule of work and other activities. You will want to be assured she is safe. And you may need to deal with any loneliness issues that arise early on. As she becomes more comfortable in her home and participates in more activities with others, you should gradually reduce your visits.

When she is stable and secure, you may want to schedule weekly visits to take her out to dinner or bring her to your home. Sometimes this will align with when support staff need time off. Maybe she has staff during the week but not weekends, so she will come home every weekend. Arrange your visits according to what works best for her and for you.

Take time to talk to her about her life and share what is going on in your life. If things are going well, she will want to share her excitement over her new life. If things are not quite what she hoped for, she may need your support. Thus, you don't want to wean visits as much as wean her dependence on you. There is a difference that sometimes is overlooked.

Support staff (such as caregivers in a group home or facility, skills trainers, job coaches, etc.) who may come into her apartment are generally very caring and honest people. However, every profession has a few bad apples. Those who work with people with disabilities are no exception, and it might even be worse because of the low salaries paid to staff. This is something you will have to be aware of as you get to know the people who are involved with your adult child.

Here are some questions to consider about your adult child's safety:

- Does she seem unhappy or withdrawn for reasons that can't be explained by separation anxiety, adjustment to her new vocational and residential arrangements, for example?
- Are there changes in her appearance (marks or bruises) that might indicate a bully at the job site or problems with staff?
- Are the funds in her budget being allocated properly? If not, could she be overspending?
- Does she have adequate food in her kitchen? If not, is she gaining weight as though she might be overeating? If she does not have ample food supply and is losing weight, some of her food may be disappearing or funds are not being spent on groceries as budgeted.

It is hard to imagine that anyone would steal clothes or food from a person with disabilities, but it has been known to happen. By monitoring these things, you might get clues as to whether she is having problems with staff.

Billy Ray has experienced this, even though he hasn't often been in placement outside of my home. As I mentioned previously, when Billy Ray was 17 years old, he was in a residential treatment program for the purpose of restructuring his medications. The program had a policy: For the first 30 days, a staff member had to be with Billy Ray if he left the facility for any reason. I drove into town to go with him to a doctor's appointment. I also got permission to take him shopping for a new wardrobe since he had lost substantial weight (probably due to the change in medication and separation anxiety).

It was an exhausting day for all of us. He had tried on all the clothes before we bought them at the store, but the tags were still on them. Billy Ray seemed tired. He needed to rest before dinner. I didn't think that he would do that with me still there. The staff person who went with us assured me that she would enter his new clothes on his clothing inventory and mark them with his name before she went home. I trusted her to do that because it was getting near rush hour and I had an hour's drive home.

When I visited several days later, he was wearing a pair of his old jeans with the belt tight to keep them from falling off. I didn't think too much of that because Billy Ray gets very attached to his old clothes. He loves to try on new clothes in the store and is eager to buy them, but frequently he won't wear them—at least not for a while. I assumed that he was still wearing his old, ill-fitting clothes for that reason.

Several weeks later one of the supervisors asked me to bring him some more clothes because he didn't have anything that fit. I asked what had been done with the new wardrobe I had bought him. The supervisor and I looked at the clothing inventory and searched his closet and the laundry room together. None of the new items had been entered into the inventory or remained in his closet. And the staff person who had accompanied us shopping was no longer an employee.

A second incident occurred as well: Billy Ray was uncomfortable taking a bath in that facility. We were encouraged to bring bath mats, towels, or anything that he was familiar with that might make it more comfortable for him. I brought him two sets of bath mats and several sets of his favorite towels and washcloths with teddy bears on them. During a visit later, I noticed that they were not in his closet. When I asked, I was told they were probably in the laundry. I didn't pursue the matter. Then one day I was given the key so that I use the staff bathroom. To my shock, his bath mats and towels with teddy bears were being used for the staff bathroom!

We have had numerous caregivers in our home to assist with Billy Ray. Most have been very honest and caring people. One who stands out in my mind had much experience in facilities and with clients who were in their own apartments. At that point, Billy Ray would be too hyper to sit down for breakfast before taking his pills. Yet, he needed something in his stomach with his meds. He liked the Danish sweet rolls from the bakery, the kind that don't stay fresh long so you don't buy more than you will use in a few days. I would go to the bakery every Sunday to buy a baker's dozen (thirteen). Billy Ray would eat one or two each morning with his pills and a strawberry Boost drink as he marched in his morning ritual. My husband, Larry, would generally take one in his lunchbox for his break at work and sometimes I would eat one. I kept pretty good track of how many were left because of the distance to the store from our country home. I sort of planned my trips to town around the need to go to the bakery.

As usual, Billy Ray and I went to the bakery following church one Sunday afternoon. Monday morning I gave Billy Ray a Danish and his Boost with his pills. He only ate one that morning. I didn't eat one because I had to leave for an early appointment. The next morning there were none to give him with his pills. Larry and I looked all over, thinking maybe staff had moved them. We even looked in the garbage because sometimes Billy Ray had thrown inappropriate things out. The staff member said he hadn't seen them. Nevertheless, only one out of thirteen was known to be eaten—and even the box they were in had disappeared from the cupboard and the trash can.

Over the next couple of months, while that staff member was with us, food disappeared a little at a time. I did some testing by buying things that I knew Billy Ray wouldn't eat and keeping track of food inventory more carefully. I observed that the food losses occurred more often when I would be away for appointments. It seemed that food was literally walking out the door!

This was even more alarming to me because this staff person worked with other clients in their own residences where the parents were not as available to supervise. It would have been much easier to walk away with food and other things in those circumstances than in our home. I worried about other clients' vulnerability. When I reported it to a case manager who arranged for in-home staff, I was told that they know some of that goes on, but they tolerate it sometimes because it is so hard to find care. Not acceptable!

It is true that pay could be better for support staff, but it is also true that many people with disabilities are already on a poverty track with low benefits. This kind of loss can be disastrous. It can impact your adult child's health, her self-esteem, and her feeling of security in her home. Thus, it is very important that parents or someone assigned to monitor assure adequate food supply, especially in the case of a person who can't call up and report she is running out of food, or even a more independent adult who may not have enough money to go to the store and may be too embarrassed to admit it.

Until you get to know the staff who are involved with your adult child, or you are certain that she would be able to let you know of problems, monitor as closely as necessary to ensure safety.

Encourage relationships that you have helped her to establish. If you invite the family you have selected as backup for special events, for some outing, or to dinner at your home and bring her home from the facility for it, her relationship with this family can be given the opportunity to continue growing. Occasionally, you can arrange to visit in their home so she is comfortable in that setting too.

Stay in communication with the potential guardian, personal advocate, and the person you selected to help maintain her story. Keep them apprised of how she is doing. Tell them about the successes she is having in her new home. And be somewhat open about concerns you have. You don't want to make things sound so bad that the person will feel he or she would not be able to handle the situation in your absence. On the other hand, you want that person to be aware of how it is going.

ADVOCACY CONTINUES

Generally, team meetings will occur much like the IEP meetings you had when your child was in school. If she is in a residential program, this will involve program staff as well as professionals from the local government agency supervising the placement and the funding.

Recommendations from program staff may sharply differ from how she was cared for at home. Obviously, some things have to change in the new environment. That is to be expected. However, there may be health and safety issues that make you uncomfortable. For example, staff may want her to take more medication rather than trying to adapt her environment or change her schedule to reduce her frustrations and undesirable behaviors. It is true that in a group setting, it is more difficult to control some of these issues with environmental and procedural changes. Given the serious side effects of some of the medications associated with behavior issues and the tendency to overly sedate some people who have used them, you should advocate strongly for program adjustments before medication increases.

As time goes on, you may see things that you know are triggers to some behavior issues; be proactive and make suggestions.

The more you can involve the person who will be her personal advocate in these meetings, the better. He or she will have a chance to observe your responses to issues that are raised—and naturally prepare to step in when necessary.

REEVALUATE REGULARLY

Whatever the transition situation, you surely hope that it works out well for your adult child. Most often it will work even though it may require adjustments in the kind of help or support she needs after trying it for some time.

Maybe her apartment is so different from your home that she needs more training than you thought she would in how to keep her place clean. Maybe you can spend more time working with her on this, or perhaps the skills trainer can come twice a week instead of once a week. Maybe she is having trouble staying within her food budget and/or is buying the wrong kinds of foods. This could impact her weight and/or her health. She might take the advice of the skills trainer more than her mom or dad's in such a matter. You should arrange for her to work with whoever is likely to have the most success at encouraging her to engage in the appropriate behaviors.

If she is in a residential facility, adjustments may need to be made for it to work out well for her. Observe how willing the facility is to make appropriate adjustments for her safety and security. Most are more than willing to try different approaches until they find what's more comfortable. Some are not.

I am by no means suggesting that you look for a reason to give up on a placement. However, if she has been in placement long enough to have adjusted to the transition and she seems consistently unhappy, is not bonding with others in the facility (either staff or fellow residents), or her health is deteriorating (sometimes evidenced by weight loss or even weight gain), you might need to investigate the placement.

Start by talking to your adult child. Maybe taking her out of the facility for a soda or some other activity would be best. Ask her if she is happy in her new home and whether she enjoys her new friends there. She may not be able to explain, but you can get a clue just by her expression or body language. Try to explore the following:

- Is she uncomfortable in the setting with more people than she had at home?
- Does she need a quieter environment?
- Is she being mistreated in any way?
- Is she able to get food that she can tolerate and enjoy?

To preserve your relationship with the facility, first take any concerns you have to the program manager or unit supervisor rather than the county case manager. Maybe the program manager will intercede on your behalf.

If you still can't work out your concerns, don't hesitate to discuss them with the county case manager. Hopefully, she will facilitate communication to resolve the issues.

If your adult child continues to be unhappy, and there has been no resolution to whatever the problem is, it is time to ask for another placement. That may not be an easy thing to accomplish because there may not be any appropriate vacancies.

Be prepared for someone to suggest that you bring your adult child home again. You'll be tempted to say, "Yes, of course." However, weigh the situation carefully. A lot depends on the seriousness of the problem. If there is a serious health or safety concern and there no other options, of course you will want to bring her home immediately.

If it is somewhat uncomfortable, but not a health and safety issue, you might consider waiting at least a short time for a vacancy in another facility. If she comes home, it could convey a sense of failure to her. Additionally, it is like starting over again.

The government agency likely has limited resources and lots of needs to address. Otherwise, the original waiting list would not have been so long.

The motivation for the agency to find her another placement is reduced when she is safe at home with you. Therefore, if it is safe for her to wait until there's an opening in another facility, it would be better.

Leaving her in a facility that is less than ideal will undoubtedly be difficult for both of you. It is something that you will have to weigh carefully. You do want her to feel she can trust you to help her when she is in a difficult situation.

In summary, you will need to be alert even though your adult child has flown the nest. Most times, things work out very well. However, when problems occur, they might not be obvious unless you are monitoring. That doesn't mean you should borrow trouble. Just be a normally concerned parent.

C H A P T E R

13

CONTINUING THE CIVIL RIGHTS MOVEMENT FOR DISABILITY RIGHTS

ONE STEP FORWARD, TWO STEPS BACK

Discrimination is the usual basis for civil rights movements. One class or another is fighting for its rights. Usually, there is intolerance and hatred. We have seen it in the fight for racial equality and for women's rights. One thing that makes it more difficult to fight for equality for disabled people is that on top of the normal kind of discrimination are the low expectations of and even pity for anyone who experiences disabilities.

The attitude about the value of someone with disabilities is demon-strated in many ways. In *No Pity: People with Disabilities Forging a New Civil Rights Movement*,[24] Joe Shapiro wrote about how pity was used to raise funds, but it destroyed the respect for disabled people as individuals with strength and abilities. Unfortunately, that is still happening. Some well meaning, but, in my opinion, destructive publicity recently has made children with special needs appear as though they are monsters—and their parents victims.

The media, while sometimes failing to cover strengths and abilities of disabled people, tend to focus on reports of parents murdering their child or adult child with disabilities. Unfortunately, this coverage may add to the view that disabled children and adults are horrible and parents are the real victims.

On Mother's Day 2006, neighbors heard 19-year-old Christopher Degroot screaming inside his apartment and tried to rescue him from a fire blazing inside. But the doors were dead-bolted, and the windows screwed shut. He was burned over 80 percent of his body and died the following Friday. According to the news reports, his parents are charged with arson and manslaughter for allegedly locking him in, setting fire to the apartment, and leaving him there to die. The report said the charge was not first-degree murder, because it hadn't been proved that the fire was set intentionally. According to the Albany (Oregon) *Democrat Herald*, November 21, 2007, Christopher's parents reached an agreement and pled guilty to criminally negligent homicide. According to www.msnbc.com, the parents were sentenced to only six months in jail each.

According to an interview with Christopher's sister, the parents kept him locked up to protect themselves from him and to protect him from others in the community who did not understand him. Again the disabled person was made to appear the villain.

The lack of coverage sometimes shows the value society places on a murdered disabled person. I remember my outrage when coverage of Christopher's murder faded, and the media in Portland picked up on a lawsuit being brought by the owner of a 14-year-old dog that had been intentionally run over by a neighbor. The neighbor had already been convicted of the crime and spent three months in jail for it. This civil lawsuit drew lots of attention because it was expected to set a precedent on the value of one's pet. There were many representatives of national and international media surrounding an Oregon courthouse to cover the story. A French magazine was even there doing a documentary on the case.

There are many stories like Christopher's that I could share. But the purpose of this chapter is to come up with as many realistic solutions as possible, not to express my outrage over the perception of our children and adult children with disabilities.

Marches and demonstrations have helped other civil rights movements. I firmly believe that in the case of people with disabilities, it is going to take more than the normal fight for rights. There needs to be awareness that people with disabilities are people of value and should be equal given rights. People need the opportunity to know them as individuals, not just people with disabilities.

Children will eventually have rights as adults, but while they are children, some of those rights are limited; children are not considered competent to make some of their own decisions. I think that is part of the problem that people with disabilities face. They are seen by many people in society as perpetual children. If they have some limitations, people may presume that they are incapable of any skills at all. Thus, the rights they should receive never really materialize.

There is a need for research to find cures. And there is a need to advocate for better services from our state and federal authorities. However, I believe the way to start is by making a sincere effort to bring your adult child and/or others with disabilities into the community where they can be known as valuable parts of the society. The community acceptance that results will make a big difference in advocating for equality.

No matter how much is done to improve awareness, there will always be intolerant people. However, if society generally understands more about why people with disabilities need things a certain way to be safe and comfortable, and if members of society are given a chance to get to know someone as an individual, it will make a big difference in acceptance.

Some people who experience disabilities find it distasteful to be watched. I have heard some compare the experience to being a zoo animal. I used to have difficulty understanding why people would feel like that, and why they wouldn't want to help increase awareness. In a recent conversation with Dr. Beth Mount, I mentioned my confusion and my belief that increased awareness is the main way that things will improve for our adults with disabilities. Beth, in her infinite wisdom, helped me see that those who feel they are being stared at like a zoo animal are those who are merely being observed. The life that I write about and have created for my son brings him into the community and makes him a member of it rather than simply someone to be observed. People in his community actually get to know Billy Ray as a person. That makes a lot of sense to me. I see it beginning to work because some are making the effort. When that kind of insight is provided, amazing things happen.

Amanda Baggs is a 26-year-old woman who experiences autism. CNN discovered her because she created a video on YouTube called "In My Language" where she described thinking and language from the point of view of a person with autism. She talks about how people are considered nonpersons if they do not communicate in traditional ways. In her own way Amanda is reaching out to explain what she experiences.

Chances are most people seeing her on the street would classify Amanda as low functioning because of her appearance and mannerisms. You might never guess that she has the skills to write, film, and upload a video that so eloquently expresses what she experiences. Dr. Sanjay Gupta, CNN's medical consultant, called her superintelligent and witty. He said in his blog that he is a neurosurgeon, but Amanda opened his eyes about autism. Sue Rubin's *Autism Is a World* video also gives a lot of understanding about how valuable someone who might be considered low functioning can be.

CREATING A COMMUNITY

In *Parenting Your Complex Child*, I introduced the idea of creating a community. The basic idea is that instead of trading at many businesses or community facilities of the same type, you could create a smaller community within the larger community. Maybe only one or two grocery stores, three or four restaurants, and whatever other type of business your family needs or likes to go to. The idea came out of my realization that there were triggers that set Billy Ray off. This included things like having to wait too long and being unfamiliar with the environment. I discovered that when he got comfortable in an environment and the personnel there got to know him, it reduced difficult behaviors.

An added benefit of that community building is that community awareness grows. Acceptance can be radically changed one relationship at a time. Your adult child can make a major impact on that acceptance by becoming an actual part of his community. You can assist with outings that your adult child either enjoys or must do for his personal needs—and that, at the same time, help build healthy community relationships.

I truly believe that as community relationships are established, even one at a time, the impact on awareness will be great. It may be as important as the demonstrations and protests of other civil rights movements. It is a new method of demonstrating—and a somewhat slower process of achieving rights. But its effects are far-reaching.

CHANGING INFLEXIBLE POLICIES

Dealing with the political bodies to end the "poverty trap" is another matter. It is going to take a united stand from parents, self-advocates, and professionals in the disabilities field to change laws and work around bureaucratic red tape. Until the impact of inflexible policies on individuals is better understood, change will not occur.

SUPPORT GROUPS

Compared to other civil rights movements relative to race or sexual orientation, parents and those with disabilities have the added difficulty of trying to advocate while still taking care of their children and adult children. This can be a life-controlling role, leaving little time left for advocacy.

Even regular involvement in support groups seems to be difficult to maintain on a consistent basis. Sometimes there is difficulty in finding a group appropriate to what we experience. If we are lucky enough to find one that we are comfortable with, it can be hard to find time and energy to attend meetings, or we are not able to find regular care for our children so we can attend.

Online support groups are becoming more and more helpful. Most prominent websites such as Google, Yahoo, and MSN have forums dealing with disabilities. This enables parents to support one another without the pressure of getting out to a meeting.

BLOGGING AND ONLINE SITES

Blogging is an especially good way to help society as a whole get to know people who experience disabilities. A blog is basically an online journal. It helps to share abilities, humor, and personality as opposed to only disabilities. Thus, it presents a whole person and his or her family/life experience.

It gives a voice to the frustrations of dealing with red tape and discrimination. Google and other avenues make blogging free (or low cost). It's relatively easy to learn how to publish, and you need not be a skilled writer or accomplished typist.

If your adult child is interested in blogging, you could assist him. The more his independent views are shared, the more others can glimpse into his unique experience. Meanwhile, you could blog in a separate journal for parents.

Recently, I received an email from a reporter requesting links to sites for parents of disabled adults. He wrote to me because I cover information relative to both children and adults on my primary blog, "Parenting a Complex Special Needs Child" (http://parentingacomplexchild.blogspot.com), which came up when he searched. I attempted to find blogs and websites for him, but failed. He responded that he had not found resources for parents of adults either, which was why he wrote me. As a result, I created "Parenting an Adult with Complex Special Needs" (http://parentingacomplexadult.blogspot.com). I feel that sharing my perspective is beneficial to other parents.

It would seem that blogging and online support groups would only be seen by parents of children or adults with similar disabilities to the author's. I have found that is not necessarily the case. The comments and email I receive based on my blogs, website, and online support group are international—and not always from parents or other family members. Sometimes they are from people just wanting to understand what it is like to experience a disability or to parent a disabled child. This too raises awareness.

It is not necessary to write volumes on your blog every day. I write when I can and sometimes will video Billy Ray in some activity. I also post still pictures. Readers seem to enjoy the video and pictures because this enables them get to know Billy Ray as a living, breathing person as opposed to my written descriptions.

Self-advocates and parents must unite to make politicians aware of what people with disabilities need most. Flexibility in policies and red tape will not be accomplished until there is both understanding by lawmakers and pressure on them to act.

I have often thought that if Congress would only realize that Social Security policies actually end up costing taxpayers more, maybe they would take a look at adding some flexibility. For example, if two people receiving disabilities benefits marry, they will lose part or all of their benefits. Suppose both were receiving funding for in-home support staff because it wouldn't be safe to be alone. Maybe one support staff would be adequate for both people. It also might be that they could help each other more and require less paid help.

As we demonstrate the abilities that people with disabilities have rather than dwell on their disabilities, our advocacy skills will have greater impact. Rather than protests and marches, helping people become true members of society will increase awareness of their value to society. We are not going to improve civil rights until we increase community awareness and acceptance.

Introduce your child or adult child to society every chance you get! It may make a big difference for him and for others who experience disabilities.

A civil rights movement is necessary to make a difference in the rights of children and adults who experience some form of disability or special needs. However, it must be done in a unique way to help society understand the person(s) before it will achieve the desired benefits.

APPENDIXES

A

Sample Emergency
Backup Plan

The plan for Billy Ray is to have his own home with 24-hour support staff. Actually achieving that plan has been delayed due to the following:

- He has experienced ongoing health-related episodes. It is desirable to get his health stable before transitioning to his own home.
- There has been difficulty maintaining in-home support staff.
- Funding for more than one shift of in-home support staff is not available as long as I am available to him.

After researching the systems for emergency services in our area, I felt that they may not be in Billy Ray's best interest. Thus, it seemed important to have a backup plan for Billy Ray in the event I become unable to take care of him before he is transitioned to his own home. Hopefully, it will not be needed but is seen as an additional protection for my son.

I have talked to a family in our church about becoming special foster parents for Billy Ray until his own home could be set up with staff or other appropriate placement could be arranged. This would enable him to remain in the community where he has relationships and to continue his support system to the degree possible.

What follows in this appendix is documentation that explains Billy Ray to friends who know him but may not have experience with someone who experiences special needs. It is intended as a cover document to Appendix B, which is a caregiver's manual for in-home support staff.

CARING FOR BILLY RAY

For the most part Billy Ray is pleasant to be around. However, his tolerance for change is limited. He gets confused about what is expected of him and has a constant need to know what he is going to do next. He loves to be busy for the most part but at times doesn't feel well enough to maintain his schedule entirely.

Depending on whether Billy Ray stays with you in your home or you stay with him in our home, you may be able to modify his schedule and procedures somewhat. If you do that, you will need to try to stay fairly consistent with your changes so that he knows what to expect.

Billy Ray's speech may be difficult to understand at times. This is further complicated by his unique terminology. For example, when he says "I fine" that means no. I have prepared a list of some of the terms he uses to make him easier to understand. That is contained in Communication Notebook II. He also has his own version of twenty questions and has answers that he has created and wants to have given to him. I have provided those in Communication Notebook II as well.

One of the most helpful tools, at least in the beginning, will be his Modified PECS (picture exchange communication system) notebook. This has Velcro strips on the front next to "I want" and "I feel." There are symbols inside the notebook that he can pull and place on one of the Velcro pieces on the cover. That way he can let you know what he wants when he can't communicate it.

I have maintained a substantial amount of documentation for Billy Ray both for the professionals involved and as training for support staff/caregivers. A full description of the documentation is contained in the Caregiver's Manual. What follows is a brief description of the notebooks included in the documentation system and where they are located.

Notebooks Contained in Billy Ray's System

1. Caregiver Manual (on the shelf of his computer desk in his bedroom)

   Contents:

   Introduction to Billy Ray

   Concepts for Working with Billy Ray

   Health Protocol

   Medication Protocol

   Safety Protocol

   Communication Systems

   Documentation Systems

   Educational Materials re: Billy Ray's Disabilities

2. Communication Notebook (on the shelf of his computer desk in his bedroom)

   Picture Schedules, including Daily Schedules

   Activity Visuals

   Billy Ray's Stories

3. Communication Notebook II (on the shelf of his computer desk in his bedroom)

   Pictures with answers to Billy Ray's repetitive questions

   Vocabulary Words (list of words he uses that might not be clear to everyone)

4. Modified PECS Book (on the shelf of his computer desk in his bedroom): Symbols to be used for Billy Ray to communicate what he wants when he can't get the words out verbally.

5. Planner (on the shelf of his computer desk in his bedroom when not in use but usually with or near Billy Ray): Briefcase-type planner cover with velcroed sheets to hold symbols.

6. Extra Symbol Notebook (on the shelf of his computer desk in his bedroom): Symbols arranged on pages by type of activity.

7. Journal/Progress Notes (top shelf of bookcase just inside office)

   Contents:

   Printouts from computer journal filed newest date on top

   List of current medication

Any printouts of medical tests or information from medical providers

Summaries

Between the notebooks, literally everything about taking care of Billy Ray should be available. The caregiver manual is written for care assistants who will come into his home, but I think the changes for foster care will be self-explanatory.

Thanks for your willingness to be there for Billy Ray in the event I can't be.

B

SAMPLE
CAREGIVER'S MANUAL

The following is part of a caregiver's manual to train in-home support staff in the care of my son, Billy Ray. You will note that I have not covered all of the issues that could be included, such as reporting time and other personnel records. This is intended to be a partial sample.

Also included is a job description that shows the characteristics and duties that will be important for a staff person together with some of the things that staff would be interested in knowing when considering the position.

CAREGIVER JOB DESCRIPTION

Billy Ray's Home
Larry and Peggy Morgan, Parents/Supervisors

Type of Position

Caregiver for mentally and behaviorally challenged 26-year-old man. Behavior issues are minimized when schedule, procedures, and health protocol (specifically pain management) are consistently followed. Billy Ray is high functioning in some areas and lower functioning in others but requires assistance. He responds very well to structure and routine. He bonds quickly to staff and friends.

The parents directly supervise this position. The parents are the employer. However, funding for the position is provided through _____ County. Training is provided by parents and the consultant.

Schedule

To be negotiated. Ideal will be a live-in with weekend coverage. Transition times are difficult for Billy Ray so typical 8-hour shifts are less desirable.

Qualifications

1. *Excellent listening skills:*
   A. Be able to listen to and put into practice all written and verbal instructions from parents, consultants, case managers, and doctors. Be willing to do as instructed by parent or consultant even if you sometimes disagree with instruction, unless it would jeopardize Billy Ray's health and safety.
   B. Be able to learn how to patiently listen to what Billy Ray says verbally and by his behavior. This takes time to learn but must be sought after.
2. *Honesty:* In addition to honesty in the traditional sense, it is very important that parents and consultants be told the truth, because it makes a difference in such things as Billy Ray's medications and general care. Occasional mistakes are tolerable. Lying to us will be cause for immediate termination.
3. *Patience:*
   A. Be willing to give Billy Ray time to respond, although sometimes the time involved can be VERY FRUSTRATING. Pushing too hard and too fast before he can process the information mentally adds to his frustration, which can bring on aggression or refusal to cooperate. The assistant must be able to step back long enough to see that his occasional confusion is even more frustrating for Billy Ray to deal with than for staff.

B. Be patient enough to help Billy Ray do things for himself and his home rather than doing them for him, even when it is easier and quicker to do them yourself.

4. *Good observation skills/honest reporting:* Observe Billy Ray's functioning, including behaviors, and accurately report, both verbally and in the progress notes, what you observe. It is not necessary for you to be able to evaluate it in the beginning, but accurate reporting helps the therapist and parent figure things out. Don't assume that if he demonstrates negative behavior you did something wrong and then omit the occurrence from the progress notes.

5. *Dependability/consistency:*

A. Dependability is even more vital than in most jobs. Although Billy Ray doesn't tell time, he has an internal clock and knows when someone is supposed to arrive. Tardiness can bring about confusion that impacts his entire day. Absenteeism is confusing to him because he believes that the person has died like his father or terminated his or her employment. Excessive absenteeism and tardiness are cause for termination without notice. That does not mean you have to come to work ill, but at least call and tell him yourself (if possible) that you are coming in tomorrow and that you are still his assistant.

B. Following through on what you say to Billy Ray is important. He often remembers, especially things you think he forgot.

C. If he is scheduled to do things on certain days and at certain times, he is most secure when things stay consistent. He gets frustrated and confused when caregivers don't follow through on schedules or change the sequence of things. He is most secure and comfortable when he is kept busy and on schedule. Once he gets off schedule, it can take days or even months to get him back on schedule.

Duties

1. *One-to-one supervision:* It should be understood that Billy Ray needs a one-to-one level of supervision. This means he is generally in view or at least in earshot of his assistant at all times. Sometimes he needs space and will go into his room alone. Other times he wants you in the room with him. You need to be in view for the most part. If he is sleeping,

you can be in earshot (for example, in the kitchen doing dishes, but checking on him regularly).

Although it is delightful for parents to find the assistant has done extra things around the house to help out, they should never be done in a way that leaves Billy Ray inadequately supervised: for example, outside tasks that take you out of earshot, so if he wakes and calls, you won't hear and he can't find you.

Duties will include tasks that Billy Ray can have some participation in. Again, there will be many times when it would be faster and easier to just do the task yourself. Billy Ray needs to be involved in life as much as possible and gains self-esteem from participating in these activities.

2. *Follow care manual and picture schedule*: Acquaint yourself thoroughly with the procedures outlined in the care manual and picture schedules. You will be given some portion of your first few days to review it. Additionally, a great time to do that is when Billy Ray watches movies or naps. Billy Ray is a slow eater, so you can be reading the manual while he is finishing breakfast or lunch.

   It is very important to follow the sequence of events listed and do things in the way he is used to. Billy Ray gets easily confused and sometimes agitated if things are out of sequence. The parent(s) and consultant will work with you on learning this.

3. *Billy Ray's hygiene*: Assistant will help with Billy Ray's bathing and will brush his teeth. Assistant must wipe his bottom following toileting, using both toilet paper and diaper wipes.

4. *Administer medications and nutritional supplements according to written schedule*: A printed schedule is in the front of the progress-notes book. Regular medications are dispensed in dose/time container. Occasional errors happen, and parents will work with you on that. Repeated errors or failure to notify parents immediately of a problem will be cause for termination.

WELCOME TO BILLY RAY'S HOME: INTRODUCTION TO BILLY RAY

For all his complexities, Billy Ray is really a charming man who is usually well liked and has many friends. He has a big sense of humor and loves to laugh. He is unique in many ways. It is highly unlikely that you have ever worked with someone exactly like Billy Ray. He has many labels (diagnoses: see below). For that reason, he requires a very special approach to every area of his care. In many ways, he is a contradiction in terms. Although it is certainly true that he wants everything done the same way and in the same sequence each time, he changes the process on his own at times without notice. Thus, this manual is written to try to explain and train you in his care.

There is some disagreement among the professionals because he does not manifest classic symptoms of anything. He has been diagnosed with Down syndrome, ADHD, autism, and bipolar disorder. He has most recently been diagnosed with chronic pancreatitis, and we are still learning the ramifications of that. We have not confirmed the reason for the pancreatitis. Initially, it was thought to be caused by a medication he took for his bipolar disorder, but recent biopsies revealed it is a different type than would have been caused by medication. This we know for sure: It causes him a great deal of pain, and managing it is a challenge. It is important to follow his health protocol for pain and agitation management consistently.

Billy Ray experienced some fairly severe agitation and difficult behaviors before it was discovered that he had chronic pancreatitis. We now realize that he has very severe pain. His reaction to it can be aggression. By managing that pain according to the protocol we have worked out, his aggression has basically stopped. He still goes through occasional meltdowns (throwing himself on the floor or just refusing to cooperate), which are generally caused by his inability to communicate what he wants or explain his confusion. If consistency in schedule and communication is maintained to the degree possible, meltdowns are minimized substantially.

Below is a summary of important issues.

1. Procedures and schedules that work for Billy Ray have been created. Staff are expected to follow those procedures and schedules instead of trying to use systems and procedures that have worked for other people. Learning to understand Billy Ray is a difficult task but vital to his success and comfort and to your employment in this position. The system presented herein should be followed consistently unless cleared with Peggy or, if unavailable, the consultant.

2. As a result of the need for consistency in procedures and schedules, perhaps the most important skill staff must have is listening skills. Every effort has been made to include as much detail in this manual as possible,

but it is not possible to anticipate every change in medications, schedule, health, etc., in this writing. If family or consultant gives instructions verbally, staff needs stop and listen fully, unless the person giving instruction and staff agree that Billy Ray needs immediate attention. Even if he does require you to follow him, you need to come back to the person giving you the instruction when possible to confirm you understood it. Additionally, you will need to learn to listen to Billy Ray both in terms of what he says and by the messages he gives by his behavior.

3. There has at times been some confusion by employees about who is the employer because the state (through the county) pays your salary. The state does fund the salary for Billy Ray's care in his own home; however, final hiring/firing decisions and supervision are made by the family with support from the consultant and case managers. Your assignments and scheduling must be arranged through the family.

   The consultant gives feedback to parents and assists in training. Questions regarding procedures can be directed to her when she is training, but she can't be here every time a question occurs. Parents should be your first step in getting answers. If they can't assist you in answering a question, a meeting with Peggy, consultant, and assistant will be scheduled to resolve needed issues and questions.

CONCEPTS FOR WORKING WITH BILLY RAY

In addition to specific procedures for working with Billy Ray, it is important to discuss concepts for working with Billy Ray and why they are necessary.

1. While Billy Ray appears charming, he needs to be related to in specific ways. His behavior is strongly impacted by approaches and ways of relating to him that would be natural for others.

   A. Over the years we have discovered (and are still discovering) what works best for Billy Ray. Procedures and schedules in the order (sequence) that work best for him are provided herein. Billy Ray may get confused when even the simplest change in his routine or procedures occurs. Confusion can cause behavior changes.

   B. Billy Ray does best if the cues (verbal instructions) that are provided in his schedules or verbally provided to staff are used rather than making an instruction to him conversationally. For example, if the written cue is "It's time to go to the bathroom," don't say, "Come on, Billy Ray, would you like to go to the bathroom?" While the cue in this example may seem demanding or formal, there is a reason we developed it. In this case, he has a bladder-brain communication problem and doesn't always know when he needs to urinate. If asked, he would likely say no because he doesn't realize the need. All cues are formulated so that they are easiest for him to understand and should be used as written.

C. Billy Ray is not very conversational. He will answer some specific questions about his activities, etc., but attempting to involve him in conversations such as what he sees outside or what is going on in television programs confuses and agitates him.

2. Billy Ray requires a high degree of consistency in his life. He will be most comfortable if staff uses as close to the same methods and schedule as possible. The order (sequence) of events does matter. Staff are expected to learn his routine and procedures and maintain them. Your input and observations will be considered as a part of getting things organized in a way that Billy Ray will be most comfortable. However, it is important that the program not be changed without consultation with parents and consultant.

Even variance in the steps (sequence) in an activity may (although not always) agitate Billy Ray and bring out negative behaviors. A very good example of this occurred a few years ago. We had been having a lot of trouble getting Billy Ray to take a bath after he came home from the treatment center. We designed an exact sequence and procedure. When I hired a staff member, I modeled the procedure for a full week and observed her doing it for the second week. Additionally, she had a picture and text visual showing all the sequence (order) of steps. A couple of weeks later I was giving him his bath on Saturday, and he became agitated when I reached a certain point in the sequence. The following day he did the same thing. This went on for three weekends. It was finally determined that the assistant had changed the order in which she lotioned Billy Ray's chest and put his T-shirt on. She was doing it that way five days a week, and I was doing it differently on the weekends, which confused Billy Ray. He was punching me out of his confusion. Note that her change was actually a good idea. The problem was that sequence is important to him because it reduces confusion. Had staff suggested the change to me before changing it so that we could have been consistent, Billy Ray would have likely accepted it with much less agitation.

3. Communication systems have been designed specifically for Billy Ray because they make his life more comfortable and ease confusion, which can cause agitation and aggression. Staff are expected to use and follow these as nearly to exactly as possible.

COMMUNICATION SYSTEMS

Billy Ray uses a variety of supportive communications systems. It is important to note that while there are many times he appears to speak clearly and understand verbal directions, he does need this intense communication support. If he doesn't use the systems on days when he needs them less, he is unable to use them on days when he needs them most. His inability to communicate his needs and wishes are the strongest cause of his aggression, so his supports are also a safety issue.

He functions best when he is clear on what is expected of him, when it is to happen, and why. He can even tolerate some change if it is done in a way that he is kept informed long before the change.

Picture Schedules

Picture schedules serve many purposes. They are like a calendar for Billy Ray. They show the sequence of events like an appointment calendar an executive might use. There is one for each day. If an activity is short, cues and instructions may be written on the schedule itself. In some cases, the detail will be too long, and the schedule will refer staff to an activity visual for the activity.

The schedule answers the question Billy Ray repeats so often, "Where are we going?" which also means, What are we going to do? Most mornings (or when he asks, "Where are we going?"), he is pleased to review the schedule with staff. Since it is used with his planner, he still has a communication tool if he doesn't wish to review the picture schedule.

The most important value of picture schedules is staff training and giving staff a base from which to acknowledge his planner each day. On the schedules will be verbal cues that you should use to instruct Billy Ray and a sequence of steps in an activity. The schedule will send you to activity visuals for instructions on activities that are too long to be included in schedules.

Figure B.1 is a partial example of a picture schedule. I have removed the pictures from this example partly for Billy Ray's privacy and partly because the pictures used in his picture schedules are not of adequate quality for publishing purposes. In the first column, the user should insert an appropriate picture or velcro a symbol that is meaningful. The sample shows the instructions.

FIGURE B.1   Example of a picture schedule.

Picture or Symbol to Use	Activity/Cue	Caregiver Instruction
	Billy Ray will wake up on his own (preferably) or at a specific time if he has appointments.	If he wakes up in a hyper or agitated state, give him 1 mg of his medication for agitation prior to other medication.
	Cue Billy Ray "It's time to go to the toilet"	Sometimes he refuses toileting first thing in the morning. If so, just go on to the next step.
	"It's time to wash your hands"	Cue him to put both hands under the water, which you have run until it is barely warm. Cue him to get soap and rub around. Cue him to rinse (needs a lot of reminding on this step). Cue to dry hands (lots of reminding or he will leave hands dripping).
	"It's time for your blood test"	Have Billy Ray sit on right-corner breakfast bar stool. Conduct test according to training.
	Take medication—"It's time to take your pills"	Prepare drink for him to take his first set of medications—these should be taken at least 30 minutes before eating.

(continued)

Picture or Symbol to Use	Activity/Cue	Caregiver Instruction
	Time to listen to Walkman and march	Since Billy Ray so frequently needs to burn off energy at this time, we are just adding this activity in. Put Walkman on and monitor him, but allow him to march. Then regroup and start with check planner when he seems tired.
	Time to check planner	Go over his schedule with him so that he knows what his day will be like.
	Feed his dogs—"It's time to feed Penny Lane"	He will get dog's dish and go the garage to get food and biscuit. You should go with him, but he is able to do this fairly independently.
	Breakfast	Ask if he is ready for breakfast. Usually he is, but sometimes wants to watch television for a little while. Follow procedures in breakfast visual for having him assist with breakfast. The balance of his morning meds will be given with breakfast.
	Cue Billy Ray to wash his hands, then "It's time to put the dishes away"	Staff removes sharp knives first. Billy Ray puts cups and glasses away. Note there will be days he will only do a few, but other days he is willing to do all the cups, glasses, plates, and bowls. If he finishes all, he can put the dirty dishes in the dishwasher if he wants (sometimes he can stay focused and loves doing this).

Picture or Symbol to Use	Activity/Cue	Caregiver Instruction
		He is starting to want to wash pots and pans again. Put squirt of soap and let him use sponge for a while then hand-over-hand finish with him. Let him rinse and then help him ensure he has all the soap off.
	"It's time to check the garbage"	Assist Billy Ray in checking the garbage—if it is at least half to two-thirds full, he will empty it. Billy Ray needs assistance in pulling the bag out of the kitchen garbage can. Staff accompanies him to take it outside, but he is able to do the task independently. He also needs help in putting a new garbage bag back in the kitchen can.
	"It's time to take your bath" (ensure that you announce it rather than ask because this is one he may refuse, and it is vital to his health because of the tendency to skin infections)	Follow the instructions and cues in the bath visual. It is very important that you follow the steps so that it is familiar to him, and he is more likely to cooperate with whomever is assisting him.
	Make bed—"It's time to make your bed"	Cue to take pillows off bed and pull the sheet tight. Cue to spread bedspread out. Cue to put pillows and stuffed animals on his bed.
	"It's time to get the meals"	See activity visual for instruction. Staff will park the van and enter the La Pine Senior Center at the rear entrance to the Center.

(continued)

Picture or Symbol to Use	Activity/Cue	Caregiver Instruction
	"It's time to go home"	
	"Let's make lunch"	See activity visual.
	"Let's watch a movie"	This could be a part of a free choice, but given his present health and the Wednesday activity, he should probably rest with a movie before going on to free choice.
	"What would you like to do?"	Staff will show Billy Ray the free choice visual.
	"Let's vacuum the rugs"	
	"Let's feed the dog"	
	"It's time to start dinner"	Billy Ray will assist in dinner preparations.
		Please note Billy Ray is more comfortable with a later dinner and going right to bed, but due to his acid reflux, it is best to put as close to 2 hours between his dinner and bed as possible. This is not always workable but is a goal.
	"Let's eat"	Billy Ray will go to the table and have dinner with staff or family.
		He is given his evening medications in a custard cup. He takes them independently.
	"Put your dishes in the sink"	Billy Ray will carry his dishes to the sink. If there is food left on his plate, he will set it on the breakfast bar just above the sink so that it can be given to the dogs.
	"Let's go watch movie in your bedroom"	He will watch his movie for a while and then usually ask for popcorn.

Picture or Symbol to Use	Activity/Cue	Caregiver Instruction
		If he doesn't request popcorn by 6:30 p.m., proceed to the next step.
	"It's time to brush your teeth and go to the toilet"	Usually Billy Ray will toilet first but sometimes he insists on doing teeth first.
	"It's time to get sweats on"	He is able to do this individually except hooded sweatshirt. Sometimes he prefers pajamas and is able to do that 100% independently.
	"It's time to put your animals on your dresser"	Billy Ray removes stuffed animals from his bed independently unless he asks for help. Often he wants you to tell him what each animal is. Staff then pulls the bedspread down like a hospital bed so that when he is ready to get in bed, he doesn't lie on it.
		There are times that Billy Ray will sit in his recliner and watch his movie for a while until ready to go to bed; other times he will crawl into his bed to watch it until he falls asleep.

Using the Picture Schedules.   When a new schedule is started or a change is made, the schedule is to be shown to Billy Ray (if he wants to look; don't push that) at the beginning of the time frame to be covered. It is also used when a new assistant is hired because it is a good training resource. Staff will have the visual available to refer to for cues and procedures to use. At the beginning of an activity, hand Billy Ray the symbol from his planner for that activity. When the activity has been completed, he can put it in the little box in this planner.

The sequence of events listed in the schedule is expected to be followed as listed. If support staff find Billy Ray reluctant or have a suggestion for improvement in the schedule, that suggestion is to be made to Peggy for consideration. Sequence should not be changed until it is agreed to.

The picture schedules will include everything that he is to do in that time frame except for doctors' appointments and other appointments. On those days use the planner symbols and activity visuals to supplement his schedule. After Billy Ray and support staff are FULLY familiar with a schedule and cues, it will not be necessary to carry the schedule IF everything is clear and the planner has been prepared for the day.

Activities that have multiple steps in sequence will often have a visual (see below) and there will only be reference to the activity in the picture schedule.

Staff will sometimes complain that Billy Ray is reluctant to follow a change in schedule. That is to be expected in the beginning. Sometimes he may be reluctant for a day or two, even becoming slightly agitated or noncompliant. As we try the schedule or activities for several days, he becomes more comfortable with them and less confused or agitated. Be sure to chart in detail what his reluctance or refusal looks like (did he throw himself on the floor, etc.) so that we can understand if it is just that it is a new activity or that we need to modify the schedule or procedure somehow. Unless you are detailed about what happens, we won't know how to adjust when necessary.

Billy Ray's Planner

After Billy Ray and his support staff have sequences in activities and his schedule fully understood and the cues memorized, he can use the planner by itself instead with the detailed schedule. The planner uses symbols for each activity rather than the detailed instructions on how to complete the tasks. Symbols are picture squares that show the person or the activity they symbolize. They are laminated and have Velcro on the back.

The planner is actually many things to Billy Ray. It is his schedule to help him to know what he is going to do. It is a briefcase that he enjoys carrying to meetings, doctor appointments, etc., because he can draw on the pad, and he likes to show off his schedule. He also enjoys putting the completed tasks in the side pocket marked "all done." When he is going to an activity for which an activity visual is used, I remove the visual from his communication book and put it in his planner so it can be read to him if he asks questions about where he is going and why.

Using the planner may seem like a lot of work. There are times that it might not seem necessary. However, his confusion comes and goes, especially when he is upset about some issue or experiencing pain. It allows him to be very clear on what is going on in his life and what he can expect. There are times that he seems not to be able to understand verbal instructions but the pictures on the planner symbols get through to him more readily.

The planner itself is a black briefcase-type notebook with several laminated sheets and Velcro strips. The white notebook entitled "Extra Symbols" contains various pictures and symbols that are laminated and Velcro backed.

Steps in Using the Planner.   As soon as possible each morning (or even the night before) gather the communication book with schedules, planner, and extra symbol book. Remove all the completed symbols from the planner pocket. Put symbols on the planner pages in the exact sequence of his schedule using the picture schedule as a guide and modifying it for any appointments not in his normal routine. He may elect to switch sequence (on rare occasions), but generally he wants to do things in the same sequence (order). If you have not been able to do it earlier, a good time to do it is when he is marching with his Walkman early every morning. Since he marches around the breakfast bar, staff can sit at the breakfast bar arranging the planner while he is marching to get rid of energy. It can also be done when he is eating breakfast.

The first symbol will be "check the planner," which can be handed to him after his marching is finished. He is then shown the schedule as laid out in the planner so that he knows what to expect of his day.

As he completes each event in his day, he removes the symbol and puts in the pocket marked "all done." The next symbol is taken. I usually cue him about the next two or three things so he has a sense of what is coming next.

Billy Ray's Activity Visuals and Stories

Billy Ray's activity visuals were created using the Carol Gray's Social Story program as a guide. The basic premise of a social story is to answer the questions about what to expect in a given situation and what to do next. Its intent is to take away Billy Ray's confusion surrounding an event and/or a time frame. It effectively eases his mind and lets him know what is expected of him.

We have experimented with the Social Story concept and created a system of visuals that works well for Billy Ray by catching his attention more fully. It can be used as training for Billy Ray and his support staff. Activity visuals contain the order (sequence) in a specific activity. These visuals will include routine activities (such as his bath routine or preparing breakfast) in his schedule as well as periodic appointments such as the Seeing the Doctor Visual.

The visuals are contained in Billy Ray's communication book (directly behind picture schedules) and are laminated because they are expected to be used and carried along in the activities until they are FULLY memorized by Billy Ray and his support staff. Visuals are not something to be read once and abandoned.

Visuals for periodic appointments such as doctor's appointments or other activities are contained in his communication book as well. Visuals for planned activities are read to him, pointing out the pictures at the beginning of the day when he is going over his schedule. The specific visual is then added to his planner for the day if you are going out of the house for the object of the story. The story is read to him again just before leaving for the activity.

Figure B.2 is the activity visual for Billy Ray's delivering Meals On Wheels activity. Note how it coordinates with Figure B.1, which is the schedule for the day he delivers meals.

FIGURE B.2   Billy Ray delivers Meals on Wheels.

Picture	Activity/Cue to Billy Ray	Caregiver Instruction
Insert picture of the step	"It's time to get the meals"	Staff will park the van and enter the La Pine Senior Center at the rear entrance to the Center.
Insert picture of the step	"Billy Ray, say hello"	The staff at the Senior Center are usually busy preparing meals. Billy Ray may have to wait while meals are being prepared or while other drivers are completing their orders.
Insert picture of the step	"Let's sit down while we wait for the meals to be ready for us"	Staff will sit with Billy Ray at a table until the meals he delivers are ready to go.

Picture	Activity/Cue to Billy Ray	Caregiver Instruction
Insert picture of the step	"Let's get the signs for the van, Billy Ray"	Staff will remove magnetic Meals on Wheels signs from the back door of the Senior Center and assist Billy Ray with putting them on the van.
Insert picture of the step	"Billy Ray, take the lunches to the van"	Billy Ray will carry the bag containing the food for delivery to the van. Staff will assist Billy Ray in placing the bags in the back of the van.
Insert picture of the step	"Take Mr. or Ms. _____ their lunch"	Billy Ray will use the blue basket to carry meals to each door.
Insert picture of the step	"Billy Ray, it's time to give Ms. or Mr. _____ their lunch, hold it up."	On occasion, a blue basket may not be available. Have Billy Ray carry the meal, reminding him to be careful. Staff must walk with Billy Ray to the door, being careful to guide him in snow and on uneven ground.
Insert picture of the step	"Be careful to watch where you are walking, here are steps. Step up." On the return, cue to "Step down."	Staff will be careful to cue Billy Ray around potential obstacles. His depth perception is limited, so these cues are important.
	No cue necessary	Staff will allow Billy Ray to greet the person to whom he is delivering the meal. Billy Ray will hand the person the meal. Some individuals are unable to receive the meal and staff will assist Billy Ray in placing the meal where they request.
Insert picture of the step	"Carry the empty container to the car"	After Billy Ray delivers the meal, he will take the empty containers from the person's previous meal *(continued)*

FIGURE B.2   (*Continued*)

Picture	Activity/Cue to Billy Ray	Caregiver Instruction
		back to the car to be returned to the Senior Center. Staff will mark on the sheet the number of return containers.
Insert picture of the step	"It's time to feed Cloud." "Keep your fingers curled."	One of Billy Ray's meal deliveries is near Cloud on Lava Drive. Billy Ray takes a moment out of delivering meals to feed Cloud a carrot. Staff will remind Billy Ray to keep his fingers out of the way while feeding Cloud the carrot.
Insert picture of the step	"Take the bag back into the Senior Center"	Upon completion of the route, the bags with empty containers are returned to the Senior Center along with the magnetic signs.
Insert picture of the step	"Great job, Billy Ray!"	When entering the back door of the Senior Center, immediately to the left there is a short hallway. The first room on the left is where the red and blue bags are placed. The clipboard is returned to Senior Center staff.

Billy Ray's Stories.   The stories are used to reinforce behaviors you want to achieve. For example, when he was gaining weight, he couldn't stand his pants up on his belly, so he kept pushing them down. He likes the western belts but was pushing them down so much that his pants would fall down. I made him suspenders with Western doodads, but he wouldn't wear them. I found a picture from his stepbrother's, "Bubba Mike's," wedding pictures that showed him wearing suspenders. I took a picture of Mike in suspenders and one of Billy Ray in suspenders and added a text box about why men need suspenders. When he asked for a belt, I read him the story, and he accepted suspenders although sometimes wore both.

Existing stories are in his communication notebook behind the tab marked Stories. Also included is the story of his adoption, which he loves hearing.

Modified PECS (Picture Exchange System).   Since he is having more difficulty "getting it out" verbally, we have created modification of the PECS (Picture Exchange Communication System) for him to communicate his wishes or feelings. PECS basically exchanges a picture for what he wants or needs.

On the front cover of the notebook there are two Velcro strips, one for "I want" and the other for "I feel." When he is asking for something that you can't understand, give him the notebook. He is to choose what he wants and put it on the Velcro for "want" or "feel." If more symbols would be helpful, please notify Peggy.

Answers to Billy Ray's Questions.   Billy Ray frequently plays his own version of 20 questions. He asks the same questions over and over. He will not accept the answer until you come up with what he is looking for. He has basically designed and refined the answers over the years. Because the names are not always clear in his speech, I have printed pictures in the Communication Notebook II with the answers next to them. He can show you the picture, and then you can read him the answer.

DOCUMENTATION SYSTEM

The purpose of the documentation system is to:

- Track responses to activities and behaviors so that we can determine what works best for Billy Ray. This will help reduce his agitation by making life more comfortable for him.
- Gather data that will be shared with medical professionals and case manager to demonstrate Billy Ray's needs for treatment and services and to ensure accurate information so that an appropriate course of treatment and/or care can be developed.
- Maintain data for history that can be provided even after parents are unavailable to provide.

All documents contained in this system have an essential purpose. The thoroughness of one part affects the ability to complete the other parts of the system accurately.

Contained in the documentation system are the following documents:

Journal Entries or Progress Notes

The journal/progress notes contain the details. The details are necessary to help us catch patterns of behavior or responses. This aids in developing strategies so that we can prevent problems or better support Billy Ray with them in the future. It will also show reactions to medications and assist the medical personnel in treatment recommendations and diagnoses.

The journal/progress notes are a balancing act. They can get excessively long if we put too much detail in the text, but appropriate detail is essential. We minimize some of that by using one-word notes where possible. For example: "toileted." This notation assumes that he went to the toilet and urinated so you do not need to write any more than that. If he had a bowel movement, you would list the bowel movement and the size (small, medium, large). If he did not have a bowel movement, just don't mention it. The only reason to chart urination is if there is something unusual, such as he could not go or there was blood or high degree of concentration, etc.

Once a routine schedule is established, you can chart: "followed schedule." For now, chart what he is doing while we are re-establishing his schedule.

Relative to behavior incidents or refusal to co-operate, journal/progress note entries should try to answer these questions:

- What happened just before an incident (this helps us determine triggers).
- What happened? Did he throw himself on the floor or throw furniture? Give the details of what happened briefly but with enough detail so that when we try to explain it in the summary or if doctors ask for more detail we can describe incident.
- How severe was the behavior?
- How long did the incident last?
- How did you handle the problem?
- What was his response?
- How did it end?

It is imperative that we have these details so that we can evaluate what is going on. Just saying "severe behavior" and putting your own judgment on what the trigger was is not enough. You can state what you suspect, but tell what he did and what he was saying or doing. Our interpretation of the behavior may not be the same as your interpretation. If you don't tell us what really happened, we can't evaluate for ourselves and assist in avoiding future events.

Charting in the journal/progress notes is very important; however, it should not be done in such a way that might potentially increase BR's agitation or leave him unattended. He will become agitated if you expect him to wait for you to chart when he is ready to go out the door for an activity. If you have not had a chance to chart something that you are concerned that you will forget, make a note on a scratch pad, e.g., tell parents, etc., and do it when you return.

At some point, you may be asked to help highlight the journal/progress notes to prepare the summaries that are submitted to physicians and other health support persons. This can be done when Billy Ray is watching a movie or taking a nap and will make preparation of the summaries much faster. Review the notes and use the color for the appropriate note. This will enable Peggy or whoever does the summary to go to the incident quickly.

SUMMARY

The summary is a document covering the period between doctor's appointments to show the doctor how Billy Ray is doing. It is intentionally brief so that the doctor has time to read it during visits. However, if the doctor wants more detail about the incidents, parent or caregiver will have the journal and can quickly look up the requested information because it is color-coded.

Peggy generally does this document; however, consultant or support staff may be asked to assist from time to time. Instructions on how to do it will be provided if you are requested to do it.

ABBREVIATED CHRONOLOGICAL HISTORY

This document explains Billy Ray's medical and treatment history. It is updated approximately each year using the prior documents for data. This history shows medications that he has tried, treatment approaches, and his functioning for a specific time frame. Peggy will do this document.

Feel free to ask questions after you have reviewed this manual and the communication system documents. What follows are protocols for health and safety procedures, which are separate documents from the caregiver's manual.

HEALTH PROTOCOL

- Billy Ray will have his blood sugar (finger sticks) tested daily upon arising and two hours following lunch. He is not diabetic in the normal sense but does experience pancreatic insufficiency caused by chronic pancreatitis. We maintain the results for the doctor.

- Billy Ray will have his first set of meds immediately following first blood sugar test in the morning. The balance of his morning medications will be taken with breakfast. See medication schedule for the list of medications. It is contained in the first page of his journal notebook and posted inside the cupboard door next to the refrigerator.

- Billy Ray takes pancreatic enzymes, which basically replace the digestive enzymes his pancreas is no longer able to make. He takes two enzymes with each meal and one with snacks. It is important to remember to take them with him when he goes out in the event he gets a snack unexpectedly. He doesn't need to take them with drinks, only with food. They are not prescribed for pain, but as his enzyme balance is becoming more regulated, it has reduced the amount of strong pain medications he needs to take.

- Pain management is a balancing act. Most times you can see the need for it coming by his whining or chewing his fingers. When it is the most severe, he will become irritable and uncooperative. It is necessary to consider if there could be other reasons for his communication by behavior. On occasion, he will ask for pain pills, but generally by the time he is able to verbalize, his pain is severe and hard to treat. Thus, we are left with a degree of guessing. He takes two pain medications _____ (milder) and _____ (stronger). If you catch signs of pain at the chewing fingers or mild whining phase, start with the milder one. There are times that he will get a sudden onset of severe pain where he will ask for pain pills or he is thoroughly agitated and chewing fingers. When that happens, start with the stronger pill.

- Billy Ray will be encouraged to eat well.
  - Billy Ray will be allowed to have as many fluids in a day as he wishes. He generally asks on his own and drinks a lot during the day. Unless he is not drinking, staff should refrain from offering him too much to drink between meals because too many fluids can affect his appetite at mealtime.
  - He will be allowed to take as much time as he wishes to eat. Staff will not rush him to finish.
- Billy Ray's food will be cut up as needed.
  - Hamburgers at home or in a restaurant are cut in half, and he is helped to pick up a half at a time.
  - Fast-food hamburgers have the paper wrapped around the burger, and he is given the entire burger at one time.
  - Meat other than in sandwiches and other foods he must eat with a fork are cut in small pieces.
- Billy Ray's hygiene will be closely monitored and carefully managed by staff.
  - Billy Ray will have a tub or bed bath every day. He will be washed using the Hibiclens medical soap prescribed by his doctor. One or two squirts per washcloth is sufficient. Too much Hibiclens can be drying to his skin.
  - Billy Ray's skin will be oiled with baby oil gel every day.
  - All areas of his body will be massaged with the oil not only for lubricating his skin but to detect new lesions that are sometimes felt before they are visible.
  - Pay close attention to Billy Ray's feet and toenails. Use baby oil gel liberally to prevent drying and then put socks on immediately so he doesn't get gel on the rug and bedding or slip on the hardwood floor.
- Family should be notified of any new lesions, preferably before applying medication so they are more visible. If family is available, treat and report to family or consultant.
- Lesions will be treated with Bactraban prescription medication.
- Teeth brushing will be done by staff holding his or her hand over Billy Ray's hand rather than allowing him to hold the toothbrush himself to ensure brushing is adequate to avoid infection and dental problems.

- Billy Ray experiences dry lips, partially from medications. A warm wet paper towel or washcloth generally removes most of the dry skin. Remove the cap from his Chapstick and cue him to put it on his lips following use of the washcloth and repeat the Chapstick two or three times during the day to keep his lips more moist.
- Occasionally, Billy Ray experiences cracks and infections in the corner of his lips. Use the over-the-counter Bactraban with zinc in the medicine cabinet only on the corners of his mouth, not his entire lips.

Note: Billy Ray's behavior has improved substantially since we began treating his pancreatitis and resulting pain better. I have left the behavior protocol in the manual for reference even though we have not had aggression for a long period of time.

AGITATION AND BEHAVIOR PROTOCOL

The most important skill in dealing with behavior is to AVOID. That doesn't mean you allow Billy Ray to do inappropriate or illogical activities (for example, those that may have health consequences) in order to keep him calm.

Agitation as Billy Ray manifests it appears in the following ways:

- Similar to temper tantrum a younger child will have. Sometimes he will yell, scream, or cry, and it is over in a minute.
- He will throw himself on the floor and sit there until he composes himself, then get up and go on with whatever he was doing.
- Sometimes he will punch or kick.
- In full escalation, he may throw anything he can get his hands on, including furniture, and become more physically aggressive.

Make EVERY possible effort to avoid things that are known to cause or escalate agitation.

Causes of Agitation

- Pain or physical discomfort. Health and pain protocol should be followed up at first sign of issues.

- Rapid cueing or overcueing. It takes Billy Ray time to absorb cues. Overcueing frustrates as well as angers him. He can escalate very quickly, and the effects may last for a day or two.

- Using too many words in cues. Be specific, not conversational.

- Change in procedures, sequence of events, or schedule, for example, the changes in bath procedures previously mentioned. It is very important that staff and family remain consistent in procedures and schedules.

- Judgment or protection statements to or in front of Billy Ray (for example, you are mad or angry). You may or may not be right about his emotions or reactions but will escalate him by stating them.

- Not being able to communicate his needs or wants so that he is understood.

- Getting off schedule or change. Even though the change or new event is something that he wants, sometimes it confuses him, and he will demonstrate that by agitation, which is more like confusion.

- Confusion about what his day is going to look like.

- Occasional memory problems.

- Items of clothing or personal property being put in a different location than normal so he cannot find them. This includes his clothes being in the laundry room.

- Being pushed too hard for compliance with certain tasks.

- Being pushed too fast to move from one task to another.

- Noise or excessive activity on the part of others.

- Clutter outside of his room except in areas he is used to. (Example: He is used to the clutter in Mom's office, table next to her chair, and master bedroom, but if it is on the dining room table, it upsets him.)

- Slight spots or crumbs on his placemat.

- Long conversations between family or family and staff even on the telephone.

- Unexpected visitors, especially people he doesn't know. An example would be salesmen or friends of family or staff who drop in unannounced. Visitors should be instructed to call first so Billy Ray can be prepared.

- There are times we are not sure what causes Billy Ray's agitation. That is rare. If you think back to the prior day or so, you can usually pinpoint something that has upset him, and the effects are long-lasting.

Intervention Strategies

Unless it is obvious what his frustration/agitation is about, say, "What do you want, Billy Ray?" (using his name helps to bring him back into focus with what you are saying). Take time to listen without speaking constantly so that he gets a chance to formulate his thoughts and respond (it's difficult for him, so if you keep saying one thing after another, you confuse him).

- If he doesn't respond to that within 2 minutes, try sitting down at his eye level and repeating it.
- If he throws himself on the floor or tantrums (noise mostly, not usually kicking or anything), try walking away for a minute (but staying in view of him or his door), then come back and try again. Sometimes he will just get over it and then cooperate.
- If parents are not available and behavior appears to be escalating into aggression, call on cell phone to alert of escalation. Follow instructions given.
- If all that has failed and the noise is getting louder or the agitation stronger, give him one tablet of his medication for agitation (under his tongue or at least in his mouth without fluids so that it will dissolve at least partially in his saliva and be absorbed faster), then try to just have quiet activity such as watching a movie for half an hour. If he is not better in 30 minutes or it comes back after only an hour, give him the second dose of his medication for agitation. If the agitation is escalating rapidly and becoming aggression, he may have the second dose without waiting the 30 minutes.
- Intervention strategies must be used before using agitation meds.

SAFETY PROTOCOL

- Billy Ray requires one-to-one supervision at all times.
  - He must be in view or nearby at all times.
  - If he requires private time or space, you can be in the living room just around the corner from his bedroom door but remain close at all times.

- Billy Ray will never be left alone outside of the house:
  - Staff or family will not leave him alone outside even to answer the phone or use the bathroom.
  - Billy Ray will not be left in a vehicle to retrieve something from the house or in a public place.
    - The only exception to this would be if using ATM, etc., and the vehicle is parked in the immediate parking space and full view of family or staff.
- Staff will always carry a working cell phone—either Billy Ray's or their own.
- If staff smoke, lighters must be carried in the pocket or carried with them, not left where Billy Ray can get them. He has not been able to light a lighter, but is fascinated with them.
- Knives and other sharp objects will not be left where they are accessible to Billy Ray. If a sharp knife is used during meal preparation, place it under a dirty dish in the sink or directly in the dishwasher after use. Note that he has never stabbed anyone, but he does demonstrate some interest in knives and has on occasion pretended to act out John Wayne movies re: stabbing. Thus, we are just careful.
- Candles will not be lit while Billy Ray is in the room and never left unattended.
- Items that are known to be tempting for throwing will not be left accessible to him. Heavy items should not be left out regardless of whether they are known temptations for throwing.

C

TEAM-BUILDING ADVOCACY

Peggy Lou Morgan

Special education services are administered by the IEP (Individualized Education Program) team. The IEP team, consisting of parents, teachers, and other educational professionals (speech therapists, occupational therapist, administrators, etc.), get together to create goals and make important decisions relative to a child's education. The impact of the decisions on a child's present and future life can be profound.

The process sometimes becomes a battlefield for parents and teachers alike. I recently saw a coffee mug on the Internet that read, "I survived an IEP," which describes what many parents experience.

During my son's early years in school, I acted as guardian for persons who experienced a wide variety of disabilities. I attended numerous meetings similar to the IEP meetings for my son.

> I could leave one of those meetings where I had been listened to, wearing the same outfit and the same perfume and carrying the same briefcase to an IEP meeting for my son. I would start out listening to the reports. The

This article was taken from www.parentingyourcomplexchild.com. It was written about children with special needs, but the concept of team-building advocacy is the same.

first time questions were asked, the sense of "How dare you question professional educators, you're only the dumb parent!" was communicated by attitude and/or body language. Comments about my lack of objectivity were common. My own requests and suggestions were rarely incorporated into the goals. I left most meetings feeling defeated and embarrassed at how defensive I had become.[25]

When conflict arises between IEP team members, the real victim is the child. Valuable time is taken resolving conflicts. A child is less likely to accomplish as much as a result. Conflict at school can affect every area of a child's life.

According to A Parent's Guide to Special Education, by Linda Wilmshurst and Alan W. Brue,

> Children behave differently at different times of the day, and the timing of their behavior may provide you with important clues. For example, if your child misbehaves in the morning before leaving for school, it could mean it is school-related and you need to investigate what may be occurring. . . . Behavior problems occurring immediately after school are an indication that something happened at school that may be bothering him.[26]

What happens at school impacts an entire family. When my son, Billy Ray, was in school, it took a long time to figure out why he was agitated before and after school. Additionally, if he had a bad day at school, he would refuse to go to school for several days. It was not only affecting our home life but my employment because of his refusal to attend school.

Children do behave differently at school than at home. Thus, trying to present the type of activity or environment a child needs to the school may be difficult. When he is expected to perform activities that are uncomfortable, the resulting behavior (for example, throwing himself on the floor in a meltdown) may not communicate what he intends. He may be saying in the only way he can (his behavior) that the activity doesn't work for him.

At the same time Billy Ray was having major behavior issues at school, he could control his behavior during a daily activity at home, feeding the horses. I frequently said to school and medical personnel, "If only we could figure out what motivates him to self-control in this activity." It seemed that no one believed me that he could do this activity.

Nothing was working for Billy Ray at home or at school. I decided to work on home and see if I could come up with answers to what might help.

I was using the program Social Stories and symbol software, eventually modifying to visuals that worked best for him. The first one I did was a Feeding the Horse visual.

During the next IEP meeting I took the Feeding the Horse visual. I wanted to share our progress at home. The reaction of the team members amazed me. Comments were made about how independent he was in that task. The director of Special Education for our district and the autism specialist made an appointment to come to our farm to observe Billy Ray in activities that were working at home.

That incident demonstrated that the school personnel were not able to see Billy Ray as I saw him. He was involved in sedentary activities that he could not handle. They saw the behavior that communicated it wasn't working for him and couldn't see his abilities due to the behavior. I could tell them but it was not as easy for them to grasp until they saw pictures and later as I provided documentation.

As Heidi Ostrom, director of Special Services at Silver Falls School District, says, "If a parent says her child can swim, but every time we try, he starts to drown, it is hard to believe he can swim."

It was a turning point in my relationship with the team. I began to try to see what they saw when they looked at Billy Ray and to try to communicate my son in ways that could be absorbed more easily. Instead of going to meetings with demands for services, it was helpful to bring support of his ability to use those services appropriately.

I also had to look at restoring the relationship with the team. The "dumb parent treatment" disappeared when the team saw Billy Ray in a different light and accepted my understanding of him. In the beginning, I had to bite my tongue when I wanted to get defensive. Getting stuck in conflict AGAIN would not bring the hoped-for results.

I looked at ways to help Billy Ray build relationships while demonstrating his strengths. For example, we didn't do the apple for the teacher or Christmas presents just to be doing it. However, when we did activities at home that would be interesting to his teacher, Billy Ray might take a picture to school to assist with show-and-tell. When we made cinnamon rolls for family and friends during the holidays, he took his teacher one with a picture showing him kneading the dough or rolling it out. This made the teacher feel special but also showed Billy Ray's participation.

If you are preparing for an IEP meeting, try to think about how your child might appear to the school staff. You might try the following:

- Consider whether she is getting the appropriate education and other services. If possible, make a photocopy of the IEP so that you can mark up one copy with changes that you think are needed in terms of life skills and academic skills.

- Make a list of any goals you would like added to the plan and your concerns about any existing goals. Resist the temptation to shoot for the moon with too many far-advanced goals. You are more likely to get cooperation if you keep the changes as reasonable as possible, at least while you are trying to rebuild your relationship with the team. Later on, you can ask for other meetings as needed.

- After you have made the goals list, think about information you need to support the changes and goals you would like in the plan. If you have pictures of your child doing tasks that demonstrate similar or beginning skills needed to accomplish the goals you will request, use them as support. These illustrate that he has some basic capability or experience to grow from.

It is not necessary to compromise every point; however, remind yourself as disagreements evolve that nothing will be solved by conflict. Your child will achieve more if the team works together.

APPENDIX

D

BECOME YOUR OWN ADVOCATE

An advocate is someone who speaks for a person to ask for or recommend certain things that he or she believes will be in the best interest of the person. As a self-advocate, you will be asking for what you believe is best for yourself.

When you're moved into a new program and attend meetings, or when you're in team meetings with the case manager of the _____ _____ (agency), you will usually be given a sheet with your rights. Take time to read it and ask questions about anything you don't understand. If you don't understand it, don't sign it until you have had time to read it by yourself or with someone you trust.

Some of your basic rights are the following:

- You have a right to be treated with respect and dignity.
- You have the right to be safe.
- You have a right to privacy. That means that case managers and others can't talk about you or send written reports about you without your permission. You may be asked to sign a release of information so that records or information about you can be shared. You have a right to say

"no" if you are not comfortable with sharing it with the person or agency requesting.

- You have the right to ask for anything you feel is in your best interest. That doesn't automatically mean it will be granted. However, you do have the right to ask.
- You have the right to healthcare according to federal and state laws.

You have many rights, and it takes time to understand them. Sometimes you will need to ask for help. Don't be afraid to ask your Advocate Assistant for help in understanding. She is your helper, not your advocate. You can make your own decisions, but she can help you understand what is involved until you get a little more experienced. You can go to her when you want to request something, and she can help by telling you where to direct your request or what you must do to apply.

There will be regular meetings of the team—usually at least once a year. You should go to those meetings and give your opinion about goals in the plan for your budget and other program goals. Between meetings, if there is something you want to talk to the team about, call your case manager and ask for another meeting. This may be because you want to change your program goals or there is something that you need, such as equipment or training.

Being a self-advocate is not always easy because sometimes there are disagreements with people in agencies or programs. Sometimes you may feel yourself getting mad because others do not understand what you are saying or do not seem to believe that you can do what you think you can do. Try to remember that getting mad gets in the way of getting your message across.

It helps to try to remember that the case manager and program manager may believe that something is in your best interest, even if you don't agree. Try to slow down and explain why you think your request is in your best interest.

Sometimes there are rules and policies that mean something you may be asking for is not possible. Sometimes doing one thing would break a rule that could cause you to lose other benefits (such as your health insurance or housing) that are important to you. If the team tells you about rules like that, it is important to listen.

If you ask for a program or something else and the team rules against your request, you can usually appeal the decision. It is best first to ask for another meeting for the team to reconsider your request. If that doesn't work, there are often appeals processes you can apply for. That means that you take the matter to another person, committee, or board to reconsider the request. If you don't know if or where you can appeal a decision, ask your case manager or your Advocate Assistant.

When you go for a meeting or an appeal, it is important to say why you want the program or item you are requesting. Share why it is good for you. It will help to practice what you are going to say before the meeting. An easy way to do that is practice your presentation by saying it to a friend or your Advocate Assistant.

APPENDIX E

U.S. Government Programs

This is only a partial list of programs. They are many government programs. Some work well together, and others may conflict (if your child receives services from one, he may not be able to get services from another). It is important to check out all details when researching the options for your adult child.

MEDICARE AND MEDICAID

There is some confusion about Medicare and Medicaid. Medicare is health insurance, which people over 65 who retire on Social Security receive. It can also be for younger people who experience certain disabilities. It may not cover all services so there may be co-payments for care. There are three components to Medicare:

Part A—Hospital insurance. This covers inpatient treatment in hospitals and some skilled nursing facilities. It also covers hospice care and some home healthcare. There may be premiums depending on whether the benefits come with disability benefits or retirement from working.

Part B—Medical Insurance. Part B covers general medical care including doctor's care and outpatient services. It covers some services that Part A doesn't cover as well. There is generally a premium for this coverage.

Prescription Drug Coverage—If you have Medicare coverage, you can get this coverage for prescription drugs to lower the cost. It is administered through private insurance companies and there is a premium for it.

Relative to Prescription Drug Coverage, note that certain companies administering this coverage will have drug lists that they cover. They are not all the same. In the brochures that Medicare sends you or you can view online, it will show which companies cover your area. Before choosing a company, it is advisable to review the list of drugs that are covered by each company, because sometimes drugs your adult child requires are covered by one company but not by another. It can make a real difference in monthly costs for uncovered medications.

Social Security has a section on its website about Medicare with links to many questions. You can also download brochures from there. The link is at: Medicare Resources at www.ssa.gov/mediinfo.htm.

Medicaid is state and federally funded care for people with low incomes or who are disabled. Because there are different policies regarding eligibility and coverage in different areas, you will have to check out eligibility with your local authorities.

Many other services are tied to Medicaid services. Additionally, Medicaid can be tied to SSI eligibility, so it requires careful monitoring to ensure that actions don't change eligibility for either.

Sometimes people who receive disability benefits actually receive both Medicaid and Medicare. The Medicaid program may actually pay the premiums for Medicare for certain recipients so that they have the additional coverage.

Information relative to Medicaid can be viewed at www.cms.hhs.gov/MedicaidGenInfo.

TICKET TO WORK

The Social Security Administration (SSA) works with many organizations that provide support to people with disabilities. Social Security also offers many work incentives to help you in your employment or educational goals. Work incentives are SSA policies that help disability beneficiaries go to work and receive benefits in an attempt to become more independent. We realize that sometimes going to work while receiving Social Security disability benefits is complicated, so we encourage you to use one of the many work incentive partners that SSA has. We offer many choices that allow disability beneficiaries to reach their goals. Whether it is working full time, part time or temporarily, it is important to know the facts. Please take the time to contact one of our many supporting organizations.

Ticket Eligibility

Qualified Social Security and Supplemental Security Income (SSI) recipients receive a "ticket" in the mail. They may use their ticket to obtain vocational rehabilitation, employment or other support services from an approved provider of their choice to help them go to work and achieve their employment goals.

The Ticket to Work Program is voluntary.

To find out if you are Ticket to Work eligible, contact the Ticket to Work Operations Support Manager, MAXIMUS, Inc. at the toll-free numbers, 1-866-968-7842 (1-866-YOURTICKET) or 1-866-833-2967 TTY (1-866-TDD 2 WORK). (quoted from www.ssa.gov/work/who_can_help.htm)

WORK INCENTIVES PLANNING AND ASSISTANCE (WIPA)

The goal of the Work Incentives Planning and Assistance (WIPA) program is to better enable SSA beneficiaries with disabilities to make informed choices about work. The WIPA program replaced the Benefits Planning, Assistance and Outreach program effective October 1, 2006. Each WIPA Project has Community Work Incentives Coordinators who will:

- Provide work incentives planning and assistance directly to SSA's beneficiaries with disabilities to assist them in their employment efforts.
- Conduct outreach efforts in collaboration with SSA Program Manager for Recruitment and Outreach contractor to beneficiaries with disabilities (and their families) who are potentially eligible to participate in federal or state work incentives programs.

- Work in cooperation with federal, state, and private agencies and non-profit organizations that serve beneficiaries with disabilities.
- Screen and refer beneficiaries with disabilities to appropriate employment networks based on the beneficiary's expressed needs and types of impairments.
- Provide general information on the adequacy of health benefits coverage that may be offered by an employer of a beneficiary with a disability and the extent to which other health benefits coverage may be available to that beneficiary in coordination with Medicare and/or Medicaid.
- Provide information on the availability of protection and advocacy services for beneficiaries with disabilities and how to access such services.

To find a WIPA program in your area, go to www.socialsecurity.gov/work/ServiceProviders/WIPADirectory.html.

SUPPORTED EMPLOYMENT

According to the U.S. Department of Labor website (www.dol.gov/odep/archives/fact/supportd.htm):

Supported employment facilitates competitive work in integrated settings for individuals with the most severe disabilities (i.e. psychiatric, mental retardation, learning disabilities, traumatic brain injury) for whom competitive employment has not traditionally occurred and who, because of the nature and severity of their disability, need on-going support services in order to perform their job. Supported employment provides assistance such as job coaches, transportation, specialized job training and individually tailored supervision.

Supported employment is a way to move people from dependence on a service delivery system to independence via competitive employment. Recent studies indicate that the provision of on-going support services for people with severe disabilities significantly increase employment retention. Supported employment encourages work, social interaction and integration.

Basic Components
Supported employment services should achieve the following outcomes: opportunity to earn equitable wages and other employment-related benefits, development of new skills, increases community

participation, enhanced self-esteem, increased consumer empower-ment and quality of life. The types of supported employment services used depend on the needs of the individual consumers. The following are the basic components of supported employment.

Paid Employment—Wages are a major outcome of supported em-ployment. Work performed must be compensated with the same benefits and wages as other workers in similar jobs receive. This includes sick leave, vacation time, health benefits, bonuses, train-ing and other benefits. Employment must be for at least 18 hours per week.

Integrated Work Sites—Integration is one of the essential features of supported employment. Individuals with disabilities should have the same opportunities to participate in all activities in which other employees participate and to work alongside other employees who do not have disabilities.

Ongoing Support—A key characteristic which distinguishes sup-ported employment from other employment programs is the ongo-ing support for individuals with severe disabilities to maintain employment.

APPENDIX F

For More Information

AUSTRALIA

Australian Advisory Board on Autism Spectrum Disorders
http://autismaus.com.au/aca)
According to its website: "The Australian Advisory Board on Autism Spectrum Disorders is the peak body representing people who have an autism spectrum disorder, their families, careers and helpers."

CentreLink (www.centrelink.gov.au) is a government agency under the Human Services agency (www.humanservices.gov.au). It has lot information about services to assist with care of disabled adults. A list of locations for the various CentreLink offices can be found on its website.

Down Syndrome NSW
(31 O'Connell Street, Parramatta NSW 2150)
PO Box 2536
North Parramatta NSW 1750
Australia
Tel: 02 9683 4333
Fax: 02 9683 4020
Email: admin@dsansw.org.au
Web: www.dsansw.org.au

CANADA

Ability Online has many links to helpful information in Canada. You can find it at www.abilityonline.org/public/code/html-links.

The Autism Acceptance Project
P.O. Box 23030
Toronto, Ontario
M5N 3A8
Tel: (416) 487-3600

Autism Society Canada
Box 22017, 1670 Heron Road
Ottawa, Ontario
K1V 0C2
Tel: (613) 789-8943
Toll Free: (866) 476-8440
Email: info@autismsocietycanada.ca
Web: www.autismsocietycanada.ca

Canadian Association of Independent Living Centres
170 Laurier Avenue West, Suite 1104
Ottawa, Ontario
K1P 5V5
Tel: (613) 563-2581
Fax: (613) 563-3861
TTY/TDD: (613) 563-4215
Email: info@cailc.ca
Web: www.cailc.ca

Canadian Down Syndrome Society
811 - 14th Street NW
Calgary, Alberta
T2N 2A4
Tel: (403) 270-8500
Toll Free: (800) 883-5608
Fax: (403) 270-8291
Email: info@cdss.ca

UNITED KINGDOM

Central England People First Limited
Eskdaill House
Eskdaill Street
Kettering
Northants
NN16 8RA
Tel: 01536 515548
Email: northants@peoplefirst.org.uk
Web: www.peoplefirst.org.uk/

Department of Work and Pensions Disability Benefits Centres
A list of local offices and other information can be found at
www.dwp.gov.uk/lifeevent/benefits/dcs/events_dbc_addresses.asp

The DirectGov website provides a list of disability benefits and links
to explore them (www.direct.gov.uk/en/DisabledPeople/FinancialSupport/
Introductiontofinancialsupport/DG_10020535).

Down's Syndrome Association
Langdon Down Centre
2a Langdon Park
Teddington
TW11 9PS
Tel: 0845 230 0372
Fax: 0845 230 0373
Helpline: 0845 230 0372
Email: info@downs-syndrome.org.uk
Web: www.downs-syndrome.org.uk

Life of Your Own
www.lifeofyourown.org

This is an organization that assists adults to create a life of their own in a
home of their own. I love its philosophy, such as this quote from its website:

> LIFE OF YOUR OWN enables those with disabilities to do the things
> in life that most of us take for granted, such as going shopping, painting,

gardening, entertaining, cycling and riding and attending community events. Everybody has ambitions and dreams.

LIFE OF YOUR OWN is committed to helping determine those dreams, respecting them and helping them to come true.

LIFE OF YOUR OWN enables people to live fully as part of the community and has the attitude that nothing is impossible. "No" as an answer is replaced with "How can this be done?"

The National Autistic Society
393 City Road
London
EC1V 1NG
Tel: (0)20 7833 2299
Autism Helpline: 0845 070 4004
Minicom: 0845 070 4003
Email: nas@nas.org.uk
Web: www.autism.org.uk

UNITED STATES

Autism Society of America
7910 Woodmont Avenue, Suite 300
Bethesda, Maryland 20814-3067
Tel: (301) 657-0881
Toll Free: (800) 3AUTISM [(800)328-8476]
Web: www.autism-society.org

2006 Disability Status Report
Available at www.DisabilityStatistics.org
Dr. Andrew J. Houtenville, Director of Statistics
Cornell University, Rehabilitation Research and Training Center
on Disability Demographics and Statistics

Disability Info
The website www.disabilityinfo.gov/digov is the federal government's one-stop website for people with disabilities, their families, employers, veterans and service members, workforce professionals, and many others. A collaborative effort among twenty-two federal agencies, DisabilityInfo.gov con-

nects people with disabilities to the information and resources they need to actively participate in the workforce and in their communities.

National Down Syndrome Society
666 Broadway
New York, NY 10012
Tel: (800) 221-4602
Email: info@ndss.org

People First
People First is a self-advocacy organization by people who experience disabilities. It has been very active in advocating for legislative changes and community acceptance. To the best of my knowledge, after much research to find it, there is no national office. They do, however, have a website for the national organization: www.sabeusa.org. The "sabeusa" stands for Self Advocates Becoming Empowered USA. There are many state and local chapters. Most are still called People First but others have different names. You can find out if there is a chapter in your area at this link www.sabeusa .org/nationalchapters.html. This would be a very helpful organization for your adult child should he or she plan to self-advocate.

Social Security Administration
Toll Free: (800) 772-1213
Web: www.ssa.gov

United Cerebral Palsy (UCP National)
1660 L Street, NW, Suite 700
Washington, DC 20036
Tel: (800) 872-5827/(202) 776-0406
Fax: (202) 776-0414
Email: info@ucp.org
Web: www.ucp.org
According to the UCP website, "United Cerebral Palsy (UCP) is the leading source of information on cerebral palsy and is a pivotal advocate for the rights of persons with any disability. As one of the largest health charities in America, the UCP mission is to advance the independence, productivity and full citizenship of people with disabilities through an affiliate network."

Thus, it is a great source of information regardless of whether your child experiences cerebral palsy.

A P P E N D I X G

RECOMMENDED RESOURCES

Morgan, Peggy Lou. (2006). *Parenting Your Complex Child.* New York: AMACOM Books.

Grandin, Temple, and Duffy, Kate. (2004). *Developing Talents: Careers for Individuals with Asperger Syndrome and High-Functioning Autism.* Shawnee Mission, KS: Autism Asperger Publishing Company.

Mount, Beth. (2000). *Person-Centered Planning: Finding Directions for Change Using Personal Futures Planning.* New York: Capacity Works.

Shapiro, Joseph. (1994). *No Pity: People with Disabilities Forging a New Civil Rights Movement.* New York: Three Rivers Press.

Rubin, Sue. *Autism Is a World* (DVD). Directed by Geraldine Wurburg. Viewing this video may help give you some ideas for adapting an independent living situation for your adult child.

NOTES

1. Peggy Lou Morgan, *Parenting Your Complex Child* (New York: AMACOM Books, 2006).

2. Joseph Shapiro, *No Pity: People with Disabilities Forging a New Civil Rights Movement* (New York: Three Rivers Press, 1994).

3. Morgan, op. cit., p. 156.

4. David C. Stapleton, Bonnie L. O'Day, Gina A. Livermore, & Andrew J. Imparato, "Dismantling the Poverty Trap." *The Milbank Quarterly*, 84 (November 4, 2006), 701–732.

5. Beth Mount, *Person-Centered Planning: Finding Directions for Change Using Personal Futures Planning* (New York: Capacity Works, 2000).

6. Declaration of Independence as originally written by Thomas Jefferson, 1776. NE 1:29, Papers 1:315.

7. Thomas Jefferson, *Answers to de Maeusinier Questions*, 1786, ME 17:8.

8. David C. Stapleton & Richard V. Burkhauser, "Introduction." In D.C. Stapleton & R.V. Burkhauser, *The Decline in Employment of People with Disabilities: A Policy Puzzle* (Michigan: W.E. Upjohn Institute for Employment Research, 2003), p. 16.

9. Andrew J. Houtenville, *2006 Disability Status Report* (Ithaca, NY: Cornell University, Rehabilitation and Training Center on Disability Demographics and Statistics, 2007).

10. Stapleton, "Introduction," p. 12.

11. Houtenville, *2006 Disability Status Report*, p. 22.

12. Ibid.

13. Shapiro, op. cit.

14. Susan M. LoTempio, *Enabling Coverage of Disabilities*. Retrieved April 25, 2006, from www.poynter.org

15. Shapiro, op. cit., p. 4.

16. Morgan, op. cit., p. 101.

17. Temple Grandin & Kate Duffy, *Developing Talents* (Shawnee Mission, KS: Autism Asperger Publishing, 2004).

18. Mount, op. cit., p. 9.
19. Grandin & Duffy, op. cit., p. 53.
20. Morgan, op. cit., pp. 182–183.
21. Ibid., p. 153.
22. Ibid., p. 178.
23. Ibid.
24. Shapiro, op. cit.
25. Morgan, op. cit., p. 58
26. Linda Wilmshurst & Alan W. Brue, *A Parent's Guide to Special Education* (New York: AMACOM Books, 2005), p. 175.

Index

ABOUT THE AUTHOR

Peggy Lou Morgan has worked with the disabled for nearly thirty-five years, including more than ten years setting up services and placements for her clients. She adopted a child with multiple disabilities twenty years ago. Peggy Lou is the author of *Parenting Your Complex Child*, has several blogs and websites, and speaks to parent groups.

Also by Peggy Lou Morgan!

Parenting Your Complex Child

Become a Powerful Advocate for the Autistic, Down Syndrome, PDD, Bipolar, or Other Special-Needs Child

"Thoughtful, thought-provoking, well-written . . . and of great value to both parents and professionals."—Bernard Rimland, Ph.D., Director, Autism Research Institute; Founder, Autism Society of America

Besides the usual parenting challenges, parents of disabled children face added obstacles that can tax the resolve and resources of even the strongest families. Peggy Lou Morgan has developed a powerful system for obtaining dramatically better care for children with one or more serious disabilities. *Parenting Your Complex Child* reflects the experience and knowledge she has gained through decades of navigating a sea of complex medical, educational, occupational, and social issues while working with disabled clients and with her own son. Morgan's unique tracking and documentation tools let parents adapt to their child's challenges, create routines that support the child's needs, communicate those needs to busy professionals—and be taken seriously by them.

Compassionate, practical, and proven, *Parenting Your Complex Child* helps parents ensure that life-changing decisions are based on the best interests of the child—and on the best information available.

ISBN# 9780814473160 Paperback $16.95

Related Titles:

A Parent's Guide to Special Education
Insider Advice on How to Navigate the System and Help Your Child Succeed

By Linda Wilmshurst and Alan W. Brue

What parents need to give their children the education they deserve.

A *Parent's Guide to Special Education* offers invaluable information and a positive vision of special education that will help parents through this potentially overwhelming process. Filled with practical recommendations, sample forms, and enlightening examples, this is a priceless resource for helping every child learn.

ISBN# 9780814472835 Paperback $16.95

60-Minute Estate Planner
Fast and Easy Plans for Saving Taxes, Avoiding Probate, and Maximizing Inheritance

By Sandy F. Kraemer

A complete guide to protecting the financial future of your family.

You can't take your money, possessions, or land with you when you die—but you can ensure that your heirs are well taken care of. Updated to reflect the latest estate and tax laws, *60-Minute Estate Planner* simplifies the complicated process of estate planning, covering what kind of information readers need to gather before they can begin. Packed with helpful forms, charts, and worksheets.

ISBN# 9780814473054 Paperback $21.95

The Net Worth Workout

A Powerful Program for a Lifetime of Financial Fitness

By Susan Feitelberg

A powerful program for getting your finances into shape . . . now in paperback!

Are your bills bloated, your savings scrawny, and your investments sluggish and lazy? This book introduces a proven program that will get your finances into shape. Inspired by the author's successful seminar program, *The Net Worth Workout* uses a subject that people relate to easily—health and fitness—to make the nerve-wracking topic of personal finance more accessible.

ISBN# 9780814474747 Paperback $14.95